BIG DAMS, DISPLACED PEOPLE

BIG DAMS, DISPLACED PEOPLE

RIVERS OF SORROW RIVERS OF CHANGE

EDITED BY

ENAKSHI GANGULY THUKRAL

SAGE PUBLICATIONS
New Delhi/Newbury Park/London
in association with the
Book Review Literary Trust
New Delhi

First published in 1992 by

Sage Publications India Pvt Ltd
M-32 Greater Kailash Market I
New Delhi 110 048

Sage Publications Inc
2455 Teller Road
Newbury Park, California 91320

Sage Publications Ltd
6 Bonhill Street
London EC2A 4PU

Published by Tejeshwar Singh for Sage Publications India Pvt. Ltd.,
phototypeset by Pagewell Photosetters, Pondicherry, and printed at
Chaman Enterprises, Delhi.

Library of Congress Cataloging-in-Publication Data

Big dams, displaced people: rivers of sorrow rivers of change / edited by
  Enakshi Ganguly Thukral.
    p.   cm.
    1. Land settlement—India—Case studies.   2. Forced migration—
India—Case studies.   3. Dams—Social aspects—India—Case studies.
I. Thukral, Enakshi Ganguly.
    HD878.B54   1992   333.3'154—dc20   92–10919

ISBN: 0–8039–9436–2 (US-hb)   81–7036–291–1 (India-hb)

Contents

Acknowledgements

This book had been planned way back in 1987. I owe thanks to all my colleagues and friends who did not lose hope that this effort would ever materialise into anything. Their patience and cooperation has been very encouraging. I am grateful to Dr. Ramachandra Guha for his comments and to Omita Goyal for her help with the manuscript.

I also owe my thanks to our in-house 'computer wizard' Sandhya Rukmini and our two typists Mary Joseph and Kamlesh Kumari.

No effort like this can be a success without the cooperation and hospitality of all those friends we have in the field, many of whose experiences we have tried to capture. Some have been named, many remain unnamed. Nonetheless they are important partners in this venture. I am very grateful to them all for making this book happen.

Enakshi Ganguly Thukral

1

Introduction

ENAKSHI GANGULY THUKRAL

Silent Valley, Tehri, Ichampalli, Suvernarekha, Koel Karo, Bodhghat, Polavaram, are now familiar names. Along with being names of major river valley projects, they have become synonymous with people's movements. Till a few years ago they were being heralded as the symbols of our country's march towards development and progress. Somewhere along the way, that perspective underwent a change.

These harbingers of progress began to be viewed as temples of doom spelling disaster for man and nature. The rivers destined to bring change became the rivers of sorrow. People were no longer willing to pay the price of progress. They began to ask: Who pays the price? Who benefits?

Dams in India are not a new phenomenon, nor is scientific irrigation. The need to harness the flowing waters of a river was felt long ago and it is believed that the mountain which Vritrasura was guarding when the Aryans are said to have attacked the Indus Valley Civilisation, might well have been in reality a huge earth or rock-fill dam. Scientific irrigation seems to have been practised since the time of the Rig Veda. The great sage, Kashyap Muni, in his treatise on agriculture gives a detailed account of the shapes and sizes of reservoirs, embankments, causeways and channels, suitable locations, etc. Innumerable other sages and scholars like

Chakrapani have made their contributions to scientific irrigation and reservoir building.

Although the recorded history of major dams in India dates back to as early as the 1700s when the Jaismand Tank near Udaipur (in Rajasthan) was built, the era of modern day large dams began in the early 1930s. This was also the time when dams were considered the symbols of technological advancement and development the world over. Not to be left behind, India too went into a sudden frenzy to construct more and more dams. Hirakud, Bhakra, Nagar-junasagar, Damodar Valley, Pong, all of these became symbols of economic progress. By the late 1980s, India had more than 1,500 large dams. These dams, it was believed, would do it all: provide electricity to meet growing industrial and domestic demands, control devastating floods and, most important, provide irrigation and water to parched lands and throats. '. . . true enough they did provide employment and irrigation facilities, moderating floods and generating electricity . . .' (Paranjpye 1988: 7).

Lands were acquired, people were displaced and devastated. But all this was in the interest of the nation and the spirit of 'national good' and 'national development' carried the people. Besides, land was not scarce and therefore relocation not difficult. Environmental and social costs were brushed aside. The few dis-senting voices of caution, Kapil Bhattacharya's for instance, against the Damodar Valley Projects were ignored (Roy 1985: 357). As Vasudha Dhagamwar says: 'no one was in a mood to listen. From Aswan in Egypt to DVC in India, no one paid heed to caution.'

With the increase in population, pressure on land increased. Relocation began to become difficult. At the same time there was a growing awareness of the disparity between the losers and the beneficiaries. A close look at the composition of the displaced population reveals, not surprisingly, that the majority belong to the poorer and backward sections of society. Even government estimates show that 40 per cent of those displaced by development projects are tribals (Government of India 1985: 18–19). In a more recent analysis, the Working Group on Development and Welfare of Scheduled Tribes during the Eighth Five Year Plan (1990–95), in its Report on the Rehabilitation of Displaced Tribals, says that out of the 16.94 lakh persons displaced by 110 projects studied by them, about 8.14 lakh are tribals (p. 43). Although exact data is not available, a fairly large proportion of those displaced also appear to belong to the scheduled castes (Fernandes and Ganguly Thukral 1989: 4).

This is not to say that natural resources are available only in areas where the poor live. More significantly, these are also the areas where the powerless live. Even though it is believed that the best coking coal of the Jharia coal belt is available under Jharia town, a small business township, it has not yet been mined, three decades after talk about mining it began. It is similarly claimed that oil is to be found beneath Gandhinagar and Baroda in Gujarat. But who will displace these cities? Is it not easier to displace the poor and illiterate?

Those who suffered the most were of course those who had lost all and gained nothing. Gradually, as the euphoria died down and realisation dawned, the muted voices that had 'expressed doubts about the claims made for dams became louder and more numerous . . . . They had made the rich richer and the poor poorer' (Dhagamwar). Questions began to be asked and protests began.

Other facts were now being discovered. Up to the Sixth Five Year Plan, Rs 15,206 crores had been invested in large irrigation projects. Taking hydroelectric schemes into account, about 15 per cent of the total national expenditure had gone into the construction of dams.

However, according to the reports of the Public Accounts Committee, 1982–83, as discussed by Singh *et al.* in this volume, of the 205 major projects taken up since Independence, only 29 had been completed till 1979–80, and not one had been completed by the stipulated target date. The then Minister of Water Resources, Shri Manubhai Kotadia, in his statement in the Lok Sabha on 21 March 1990 said that as many as 16 cases of failure of large dams have been reported in the country. Of them, 13 were reported in the post-Independence era and 11 had reportedly failed within five years of completion.

The 1960s and 1970s saw the emergence of agitations in Maharashtra against the large number of dams that had been built in the state (NCHSE 1986: 18). This led to the formulation of The Maharashtra Project Displaced Persons Rehabilitation Act in 1976. Slowly, similar agitations began to take place in other parts of the country as well. In 1970, about 4,000 persons affected by the Pong dam in Himachal Pradesh marched to the dam site and stopped work for 15 days. The Pong Dam Oustees' Association is still fighting for its rights (Bhanot and Singh). Of the 2,180 families displaced by the Bhakra dam in 1942–47, only 730 had been resettled till as recently as 1988. And that too, after they had submitted a petition to the Lok Sabha in 1978–79, two decades after they had been displaced. A mass movement against the Koel Karo dam and a writ petition in the Supreme Court in 1984 temporarily put a stay on construction work. An agitation against the Bodhghat project also resulted in putting a stop to construction.

But these agitations were project specific and therefore dispersed and localised. Even though opposition to large dams had become a worldwide phenomenon, it was with the Silent Valley, and the controversial Narmada and Tehri projects that international attention was focused on India.

Between 1986 and 1989 MARG conducted studies on the Sardar Sarovar oustees of Madhya Pradesh. It was during this time that we realised just how little information was available on the displacement and rehabilitation of people due to such projects. In order to better understand the situation of the oustees it seemed important to look in some detail at the experiences of those who had been affected in the light of the policies that governed their rehabilitation. It was in an attempt towards understanding the impact of displacement and the nature of rehabilitation of other dam oustees that this book was born.

The causal factors of displacement are manifold and complicated, some visible, others not. The most visible cause of displacement is due to the acquisition of land for development projects. In this volume, we have concentrated upon displacement caused by dams, as this, amongst all developmental projects, is the single largest cause of displacement. We have also focused on those who have been directly displaced by the projects and hence are in need of relocation by the government.

The decision to include the case-studies on Hirakud, Nagarjunasagar, Pong and Ukai rested on both their geographical location and the years in which they were undertaken.

Hirakud was the first major project undertaken in independent India, work on which began in the 1940s. It is also an example of a dam in the eastern part of the country. This study was conducted in 1987. Nagarjunasagar is an example of a project in the southern part of India undertaken in the 1950s. It is also an example of what the Government claims as a successful rehabilitation exercise.

Pong is a project in the north of India begun in the 1960s. Although construction was completed in 1974, the rehabilitation of its oustees is still not complete. It is also an example of an interstate project. The Ukai project in the western part of India began in the 1960s and has certain interesting features. A large portion of the submergence zone had once been part of the Dhule district of Maharashtra. After the project, this area was transferred to Gujarat where the oustees were offered resettlement.

It is true that this choice of projects on the basis of a division of the country into four geograpical zones is not fully representative of the area as a whole, especially because the problems faced by each state, or even areas within each state, are specific to it. But given our time and resource constraints we believed that the choice of projects on the basis of this rough geographical division might help provide an insight into the problems faced by the oustees. It could also help us examine the policies that have governed the rehabilitation of the oustees in various parts of the country at different points in time.

The study of the Baliraja dam project in the Sangli district of Maharashtra was undertaken because it is an example of a dam built by the people themselves.

All the papers included in this volume, except the one by Singh *et al.*, are written either by members of MARG or by persons requested to write them on behalf of the organisation. The paper by Singh *et al.* has been included in this book because it throws light on the shortcomings of the evaluation process of our irrigation projects and suggests changes that are necessary so that many of the pitfalls that have become so much a part of dam projects and have been discussed in the case-studies can be avoided in future.

MARG undertook two studies, on the oustees of the Pong dam and the Nagarjunasagar dam. The study on Hirakud dam by Philip Viegas and on the Baliraja dam by Macchindra D. Sakate were commissioned by MARG. The paper on the Ukai Project written by Kashyap Mankodi for MARG is based on an earlier study conducted by him and Tanushree Gangopadhyay on the social and environmental cost of the Ukai dam project as well as on subsequent visits he made to the area.

In the case of the studies undertaken by MARG or those undertaken on behalf of MARG, i.e., the studies on Hirakud and Baliraja, we provided a schedule or checklist of questions which delineated the areas on which information was to be collected. In most cases the authors have endeavoured to adhere to the schedule, although at times this proved difficult.

In the case of projects like Hirakud or Nagarjunasagar, for instance, which are more than 30 years old, it was difficult to trace the relevant documents. Most of the officials who had been involved in the projects had either retired or been transferred, many were no longer alive. The same applied to the oustees. Many were no longer there. Some had died and others had been forced to migrate. Among those still available, some had grown too old to remember, while those who had been young at the time of displacement did not recall the events of the past. They were only able to recount what they had heard from their elders. They were however, living examples of what befalls the next generation of the displaced. Time being the best healer, memories of their experience had dimmed and the researchers had to probe very deep to revive them. Besides, there was the problem of language. The researchers had to depend on translators to communicate with the oustees, which always diminishes the quality of the interview.

Our study on Pong proved the most difficult of all. Information for this study took two years (1987–89) to collect. This, after numerous visits to various places, some proving to be futile. Although this is a fairly recent project and rehabilitation work is not yet complete, it was very difficult to trace the documents. Once traced, the officials refused to part with them, as a result of which many of our sources have had to be kept anonymous. Meetings with the oustees had to be held both in the villages of Himachal Pradesh and the rehabilitation sites in Rajasthan.

In the event, although our work on compiling these case studies began in 1987, it was only in 1990 that all the reports could be completed.

We are aware that this effort too, is like most endeavours of this nature, a post-mortem. But we hope that it will contribute to the on-going debate on displacement and rehabilitation in the country and help to critically examine future projects in the light of past experiences, which were a result of an absence of adequate planning and proper implementation.

Any involuntary dislocation, be it due to natural causes, political unrest or developmental projects, is bound to be painful. But while in the case of displacement due to natural calamities and political unrest there is a possibility of being able to return to the original place of domicile and to restore, to some extent, one's original way of life, in the case of project related displacement, this possibility does not exist.

Persons who are uprooted and rehabilitated in another place have to undergo the entire process of resocialisation and adjustment in an unfamiliar environment. Traditional social relations and community networks break down as a result of displacement, leading to physical and psychological stress. It also leads to economic disruption, often resulting in impoverishment and insecurity. Inadequate and unplanned resettlement, with little or no share in the benefits from the project that has caused this displacement, further increases the misery of those affected. A hostile host population in the new area only serves to aggravate the trauma. Fall out in the form of alcoholism, gambling, prostitution, and even increased morbidity, is not unknown.

A distinct pattern emerges from these studies of displacement and rehabilitation.

The first striking feature is an abysmal lack of information. The Detailed Project Reports that sometimes run into volumes contain copious information on the project, perhaps even down to the last ounce of mortar used. But these reports contain minimal information concerning the displaced persons. The Directory of Dams, brought out by the Central Water Commission and the Irrigation and Power Board, graphically describes every minute detail about the project but makes no mention of the people affected. Rehabilitation is not their primary task. Theirs is to provide irrigation and water. In the absence of any other authority, they do undertake the responsibility, of relocation, on sufferance as it were. Collecting official information on displacement and the rules that govern rehabilitation is therefore itself an uphill task. Arriving at an estimate of the magnitude of the problem is even more difficult. In the absence of adequate data the various estimates available seem to be based largely on surmises and conjecture. Fernandes, Das and Rao (1989: 80) have estimated the number of persons displaced in the last four decades at 18 million. Mankodi states that although no reliable statistics are available, the number of displaced could be anywhere between two and more than 20 million (1989: 150). Another estimate puts the number of persons affected directly or indirectly by irrigation projects alone over the past 40

years at 20 million, of whom, only 25 per cent have been rehabilitated (Bhaskara Reddy 1989: 469–79).

However, these estimates exclude a very large section of the
affected population: those who are not directly affected due to the
acquisition of their lands, but indirectly, due to the changes in the
land-use pattern, as a consequence of the project. These persons
too are often forced to leave the area after having lost their source
of livelihood or their access to the biomass resources on which they
depended. Thus, they too are thereby displaced.

Whether the project is major, medium or minor, whether the
numbers involved are large or small, the attitude of the authorities
towards the affected is the same—apathetic and negligent. Since
very little effort is made to involve the oustees, they remain
ignorant and uninformed about the project and their future. The
land surveys are incomplete and more often than not inaccurate,
as are the estimates of the numbers affected. This has been illus-
trated by the studies on Hirakud and Nagarjunasagar.

The construction of the Nagarjunasagar project began in 1955.
The socio-economic surveys were conducted after 1957 and continued till 1965. The displacement began in 1959, well before the
surveys were complete. As Singh and Samantray write: 'it indicates
that the affected population was not given any importance when
the dam was initiated'. The first phase of submergence of the
Sardar Sarovar oustees of Madhya Pradesh will begin in 1992. In
1990, the land surveys of these villages was still underway.

These are examples of large projects. The experiences of oustees
in smaller projects like the Chaskaman project in Maharashtra, or
Daman Ganga in Gujarat, were not very different. The potential
oustees of Nisarpur in the Kukshi tehsil of Madhya Pradesh met
an oustee from the Daman Ganga project, Shri D.K. Phatakia,
when they visited a rehabilitation site at Malwa Toomb in Gujarat.
He had been displaced in 1974 but had not been rehabilitated. He
had once been a fairly prosperous farmer and showed his visitors
photographs of his old life. He had even filed a case in the
Supreme Court which he had later withdrawn when he was assured
by the government that his grievances would be looked into and
his demands met. Nothing happened. He had himself purchased
the plot on which he was presently living. He asked the visitors
that if, in spite of being prosperous, this was his state, what would

be the plight of the other oustees, most of whom were tribals? 'Look at me, do not trust the government,' he said (MARG 1991).

The oustees of Chaskaman in Maharashtra had organised themselves under the leadership of Baba Adhav, one of the most eminent and respected social workers in Maharashtra. They had been in constant touch with the government over the problem of displacement and rehabilitation. Despite this, however, they did not know why the dam site had been changed, nor were they clear about their rehabilitation rights.

The trauma of displacement begins well before the process itself actually takes place. As soon as the project is announced, all development work in the area comes to a halt. No one wants to invest in land that is to be submerged. Banks refuse to give loans, no new civic amenities like schools and health centres are constructed. Even the withdrawal of existing facilities is not unknown. Since the gestation period of dams is much longer than that of other projects, the suffering of the people is all the more intense. The examples of the potential oustees of the Narmada and Tehri projects are cases in point. 'I have been hearing about the dam since my childhood. Since they declared that the dam is to be constructed here, they have not built anything for us. No hospitals, no schools for our children, no roads and no buses to travel,' Gobind Prasad, a farmer from Bijapur who is to be displaced by the Indira Sagar dam in Punasa (Madhya Pradesh) is quoted as saying (anonymous 1988: 1264). The psychological preparedness for displacement is never given consideration. What happened in the case of the Nagarjuna oustees is bound to result. Even though they had been informed about their impending displacement, they did not vacate their land. Finally, many had to be forcibly evacuated by the army. In the case of the Rihand project, the oustees were not informed in advance. When the waters were released they had, literally, to run. In the case of the Koyna dam too, people were completely unprepared. '. . . there was no time to bring our household goods. The waters rose so quickly that we had to run for life. The water came and everyone cried run! run!' (Karve and Nimbkar 1969: 63). So also were the oustees of the Pong dam caught unawares.

Land for projects is acquired under the Land Acquistion Act, 1894, displacing the people occupying that land. This Act, however, does not provide for resettlement. The rate of compensation, as also its nature, are decided project-wise. As a result, the oustees are often dispensed with, with the minimum cash compensation.

There is no national policy or law for rehabilitation. The resettlement of the oustees is governed by various policies and rules of the concerned state governments or those formulated for the project. Resettlement is, therefore, most often *ad hoc* and piecemeal. Only two states, Maharashtra and Madhya Pradesh, have laws governing the rehabilitation of project-displaced persons (The Maharashtra Project Displaced Persons Act, 1976 and the Madhya Pradesh Pariyojana ke Karan Vishthapit Vyakti [Punahsthapan] Adhiniyam, 1987). Other states and government departments have their own policies. The rehabilitation of the Nagarjuna oustees, for instance, was in accordance with one government order, two memos and a state amendment to the Land Acquistion Act, 1894. In the case of the Ukai project, as Mankodi shows, there was no well-planned policy to govern the relocation and resettlement of oustees but a series of executive fiats were formulated to address problems as they arose.

Since little or no effort was made to consult those affected, the compensation was both inadequate and inappropriate. In the case of Hirakud, for example, the oustees found themselves totally at a loss. They had no idea about how their lands had been evaluated or their compensation calculated. Compensation for land had been awarded to only those who had *pattas* or legal documents to prove their ownership. As a result, many were left out even though they had been cultivating the land for generations (Veigas). This is only one example. Cash in the hands of the poor, especially the tribals who have little or no exposure to the outside world, has very little meanir . Experience shows that they took what was offered and 'it ran through their fingers like water in a sieve' (Dhagamwar). Philip Viegas, during the course of his study on the Hirakud dam oustees, found that unused as they were to so much money, the tribals fell prey to petty businessmen selling colourful trinkets and consumer items like transistors and watches, or lost their money in gambling and on liquor. This was also the experience of the oustees of the Koyna project in the 1960s, and more recently, of the Kutku dam oustees. 'It was an error to hand over thousands of rupees to people who had hardly handled cash at all. Now, a number of years later, a large majority of the displaced are still without a roof over their heads' (Karve and Nimbkar: 1969: 72).

The Nagarjunasagar oustees told us that they had been promised land for land, along with irrigation facilities and house plots. However, as per the rules, they received only five acres of dry land. This was not in the command area and they were not entitled to irrigation facilites from the project that took away their land. The Hirakud oustees found that their rehabilitation sites were a great distance away, badly connected and totally unprepared for resettlement. It is estimated that no more than 11 per cent of the oustees decided to settle in these camps. The others preferred to find their own alternatives.

If the project involves more than one state, an entirely new set of problems arises. In such cases, the plight of the oustee is even worse because even though each state wants the maximum benefits of the project, neither wants to share the responsibility of rehabilitating the people consequently displaced, (Ganguly Thukral 1989: 44). The case of the Pong oustees is a good example. The states of Rajasthan and Himachal Pradesh seem intent on playing a game of ping-pong with each other, forcing the oustees to shuttle between the two states looking for redressal in vain. While many were not rehabilitated, others, having lived their lives in the hills of Himachal Pradesh, found themselves unable to cope with the deserts of Rajasthan where they had been offered resettlement. The affected population had been offered relocation in the command area where the promised waters of the project were destined to reach. But, in the meanwhile, they found the conditions so inhospitable and alien that many were forced to return to Himachal Pradesh. Besides, the stringent and impracticable Colonisation Rules of the Rajasthan government made it difficult for the oustees to retain their land.

Since rehabilitation is undertaken project-wise by independent authorities who have little or no coordination between them, the same people find themselves displaced more than once, each time as the result of a different project.

Singrauli, as a symbol of unplanned development, has been much written about, discussed and criticised. The situation there has been likened by many to the lower circles of Dante's inferno. Multiple displacement, with each subsequent displacement leading to a further degeneration of life and environment, has become the hallmark of Singrauli—the area that Nehru had envisioned as the Ruhr Valley of India.

The first lot of people were displaced by the Rihand dam in the

1960s. Subsequent projects in the form of mines, railway lines, thermal power plants and industries, and the efforts of the Special Area Development Authority (SADA), all of which came up within a 20 km radius of the Rihand reservoir, forced the displaced to undergo the process repeatedly, sometimes as many as five times. Their displacement might well continue.

The experience of Singrauli was repeated in Korba. People were displaced when land was acquired for the Hasdeo Bango dam. Subsequently, land was acquired for open-cast mining, setting up of thermal power plants, and aluminium and fertiliser industries. As a result, people were displaced more than once. Now again people in the area are faced with displacement because of the Rakhad dam project and more open-cast mines that are to be set up in future.

Some of the Tehri dam oustees had been rehabilitated at Jolly Grant site near Dehradun. The government now proposes to acquire the land from the resettled oustees to extend the Dehradun airport. They, too, are to be displaced yet again.

Surely the experience of displacement and relocation once in a lifetime is traumatic enough without forcing the oustees to repeat it? That the same people have to undergo this trauma more than once reflects the government's complete lack of understanding of let alone planning for the problem.

What happens to the displaced who are not relocated? 'It is small wonder that a substantial number among them are reduced to a relentless struggle for survival.' What Bhanot and Singh observe about the Pong oustees applies to all those in a similar situation. Without resettlement, unless they are rich, or big landlords or politically powerful, the displaced find themselves in a state of pauperism. They are forced to join the legions of migrant labour flocking to urban slums in search of work in the cities.

The Bhil oustees of Ukai are forced to migrate seasonally in search of work, most of them as labourers on the sugar-cane plantations. At other times they are unemployed. While shooting a film on displacement, *Baste Ujad te: Kal Ki Talash Mein*, we interviewed Hirji Bhai, an oustee now resettled in village Tokarwa in Gujarat. Describing their situation he said, 'all the work left for us today is brewing country liquor, fishing and thieving . . . .' He was angry because he and others like him had lost all and gained nothing. In despair he said, 'we have given our blood for those in the command area . . .' Mankodi's study on Ukai attempts to document the situation of the oustees. He finds that more than a decade after the completion of the project, there was nothing for the displaced to occupy themselves with. It is not without reason, therefore, that Shri Ramesh Desai, a Sarvodaya leader, who, in the 1970s, had convinced the Ukai oustees to sacrifice their lands for the national good, had become one of the most vociferous anti-dam activists towards the end of his life. The Nagarjuna oustees are faced with a similar situation. The history of rehabilitation and resettlement is replete with such instances of displaced people being forced to join the ranks of migrant wage labour, often falling into bondage, crime or penury.

Why the Problem?

Given the growing needs of our society, it is true that not all projects can be brought to a halt. But it has become imperative to put much more thought into the planning process so that displacement is kept to the absolute minimum and, if possible, avoided.

Before undertaking any project, therefore, it is extremely important to conduct an extensive viability study, taking into account all the social, environmental and economic costs of the project. The paper by Singh *et al.*, stresses the importance of this aspect. However, according to the authors, it is the very method of evaluation which has been conducted so far, that has lost its credibility. And this, because the project authorities have failed to evaluate the social and environmental cost. New methods and new parameters of evaluation will have to be drawn to be able to make a more holistic evaluation. The study on the oustees of the Ukai dam shows the increase in social evils such as alcoholism and prostitution; the increase in the death rate in Parvaeta in Gujarat, where the Narmada oustees have been resettled, shows that the fear of increased morbidity was not unfounded.

There are different sets of people who are affected by any project:

1. Those who are directly displaced by the project due to the acquisition of their lands and properties. Among them are

people from whom only a part of their property is acquired, and who, although faced with acquisition, are not entitled to resettlement.

2. Those who are not faced with direct acquisition but are nonetheless affected due to changes in the land-use pattern as a result of the project. These are the project-affected persons. Among them are:

   a Those who have lost access to the natural resources on which they traditionally depended. Left with no alternative they are forced to move out of the area and are thereby displaced.

   b Those who are affected because the people on whom they depended for their livelihood are no longer there. For example, Harsud and Nisarpur towns in Madhya Pradesh are to be submerged due to the Narmada Sagar and Sardar Sarovar dams. Both these towns serve as important market centres for the villages from neighbouring areas where they sell their goods and services. The market economy of the entire area is bound to be affected by the submergence of these towns.

   c Those who are affected by the environmental consequences resulting from the project. For example, impoundment of water in reservoirs is known to cause earthquakes. The experience of the Koyna and Morvi dams is too recent to be forgotten. Waterlogging and increase in salinity due to the construction of dams is also well established (Goldsmith and Hildyard 1989).

This is not to say that all these sections of the population need relocation. Rather, the phenomenon of displacement needs to be looked at and understood in a much wider context than mere physical dislocation. The larger implications of displacement have to be kept in mind when assessing the viability of a project in order to tackle the problem better.

One of the most important factors that tends to be overlooked when a project is initiated is people's opinion. Do they want it? Do they see it as a solution to their problem? The study of the Baliraja dam is an example of how it is possible to construct a dam for irrigation with the full participation of the people and resulting in no displacement. Of course, an experiment like Baliraja cannot always provide the solution. The solutions have to be area and situation-specific and based on the needs of the people.

Only an exhaustive exercise to establish the necessity of the project can justify its initiation.

What Should Rehabilitation Be?

It is by now well-established that, 'by its very nature, displacement is a disruptive and painful process. Economically and culturally . . . it creates a high risk of chronic impoverishment that typically occurs along one or several of the following dimensions: landlessness, joblessness, homelessness, marginalisation, food insecurity, morbidity and social disarticulation' (Cernea 1990: 20).

According to the Oxford Dictionary, rehabilitation is 'to restore to original'. According to the Chamber's dictionary, it is 'to reinstate, to restore to former privileges, rights,rank etc.'. But given the present pressure on land, scarce natural resources and the changing needs of the people, one cannot but be sceptical about the feasibility or desirability of merely restoring people to the 'original state'. Hence, the demand has to be for 'adequate and appropriate resettlement'. Relocation of the Pong dam oustees from the hills of Himachal Pradesh to the deserts of Rajasthan on sites totally unprepared for resettlement, or cash compensation to tribals completely unaccustomed to handling money, are perfect examples of 'inappropriate resettlement'.

As already mentioned, the problems of displacement begin well before the actual dislocation takes place. The knowledge of future displacement is enough to instil in the people a feeling of insecurity and a fear of the unknown. It is not only the psychological aspects that need to be tackled but also the physical aspects, the withdrawal of civic amenities, for instance. Displacement in the future should not mean a damaging break with the present. It has to be ensured, as far as possible, that a certain continuity is maintained and that the people are equipped to handle their future displacement.

Special efforts have thus to be made to prepare the prospective oustees. Their involvement from the outset in the planning of their resettlement, providing them with more information about the dam, showing them the site, etc., are all important ways of preparing them for the nature of change. Appropriate resettlement, apart from preparing them psychologically for their displacement, would ensure that they play a part in their own destiny. Our studies on the oustees of the Sardar Sarovar in Madhya Pradesh revealed that not only were the people uninformed but that they were often deliberately misinformed about the project and their future.

Along with preparing the oustees for displacement, an equal effort needs to be made to prepare the host population so as to protect the oustees from the hostility they usually face in their new environs. It is important that the host population not view the new entrants as a threat but be willing, instead, to share the available resources with them. Many displaced people have had a bitter experience with their hosts. In the case of the Pong dam oustees resettled in Rajasthan, for instance, not only were they harassed, beaten up and their lands grabbed, many of them were even murdered. As a result, many of the settlers returned to Himachal Pradesh.

The Government of Gujarat began anticipating such reactions, and made special efforts to help integrate the Madhya Pradesh oustees, now resettled in Gujarat, with assistance from local voluntary organisations. However, it is as yet too early to assess the outcome of these efforts.

There are certain sections of the affected population who need extra attention: landless labourers and artisans, for instance, who lose their livelihood as a result of development and displacement. Until recently they were not entitled to any compensation except for house plots. Although the Gujarat government is offering 5 acres of land to all the oustees of the Sardar Sarovar Project, it has little meaning for those of the landless not used to agriculture. They will need special assistance to enable them to take up their original occupations, or be trained in new fields.

Although women form a large proportion of the displaced, very little or no attention is paid to them by both the authorities concerned and the displaced male population. During the course of our meetings with the oustees, whenever we put a question to the women, the men would ask, 'why do you want to talk to her, what does she know?' But on speaking to the women we realised just how severely they were affected and how little their fears were appreciated, particularly by the men, whose main concern was the loss of their lands.

The women are responsible for collecting food, fuel, fodder and water in most of rural India. It is an arduous task even in normal circumstances, given the present conditions of deforestation and environmental degradation. They were particularly anxious about how these needs would be met after displacement. Experience shows that their fears are not ill-founded. In Singrauli, the women complained that life prior to displacement was hard, but there was water available from the river and fuel and fodder could be got from the forest. Now, the dam had monopolised the water, which in any case was too polluted to be used, and mining operations had taken over the forest. Even the wells had been polluted by coal and cement dust and gravel. Since no alternative sanitation facilities had been provided, their lives were made all the more complex. We have seen that even in the case of the oustees of the Sardar Sarovar dam who have been resettled in Gujarat, fuel and fodder for cattle is a major problem.

Because women in India are much less mobile than men, the breakdown of village and social units affects them much more severely. The fact that she might be leaving relatives and friends behind, or may never again meet her daughter who is married into a village which will not be displaced, is a great cause of concern for the woman, a fear that cannot be easily brushed aside.

Very few women own property or have land *pattas* in their name. They are, therefore, seldom entitled to compensation. It is the adult male who is considered to be the head of the family in the case of joint holdings. The Narmada Water Disputes Tribunal (NWDT) in its Award defines family to include husband, wife, minor children and other persons dependent on the head of the family, like a widowed mother. The Award also stipulates that every major son will be treated as a separate family. What then happens to a woman who is the head of the family or a single woman or a widow with minor children? One cannot help but wonder if it is a mere coincidence that Gajaraben, a widowed mother of two children whose land in Mukhari village in Gujarat is to be submerged, has been compelled to live with her father, Shankar Moti, and is yet to get her share of land! The NWDT is only one example of the government's discriminatory policies. Interpreters of the law would explain that in law 'man embraces woman'. Nevertheless, it is disheartening that, even today, our planners regard women as the mere dependents of men.

There is an urgent need for more holistic developmental planning, keeping in mind the social and environmental needs of the people and the various uses to which the land might be put in future. In this way, multiple displacement can be avoided as it not only means hardship for those subjected to it, but also heavy investment of scarce resources in displacing and rehabilitating the same people more than once.

It is true that those displaced from their lands want land in return for what they have lost, and justifiably so. But studies indicate that even if land is available, mere allocation is not enough. Where land was allotted to the oustees, as in the case of the Koyna and Nagarjunasagar projects, they were unable to subsist on the land beyond one or two generations. 'With the rising population and pressure on land, we see a lot of people being forced to take other jobs, but they are handicapped in the urban areas due to their lack of education and training' (Karve and Nimbkar 1969: 72). Without alternative skills, only menial jobs that are the lowest paid and most hazardous are open to them.

With the passage of time, less and less land is available. While the government promises land, it finds itself unable to provide it. As a result, in most cases, the land allotted is much less than the amount lost. Most of those affected are not even allotted the bare minimum. In the case of the Tehri project, the oustees have been promised a maximum of 2 acres of land, regardless of the amount lost. The Sardar Sarovar oustees have been promised a minimum of 5 acres of land. The government's ability to fulfil these promises is seriously in doubt. In the case of the Sardar Sarovar oustees, the Maharashtra government has openly admitted that it does not have revenue land for rehabilitation and has therefore released 2,500 acres of forest land. While one has reservations about the wisdom of releasing already diminishing forest lands for resettlement, much of this forest land too is encroached upon and therefore not unoccupied. The Madhya Pradesh government also admitted its inabilty to find land for everyone, even in 1984 (Narmada Control Authority 1984: 7). It is therefore telling its oustees that if they want to be rehabilitated, they must go to Gujarat.

It is worth noting that the process of rehabilitation is itself leading to more displacement. The Gujarat government, in order to rehabiltate Sardar Sarovar oustees, is buying private land from absentee landlords willing to sell. But in the process labourers, who were engaged in these fields for years, have been rendered jobless, as the oustees who have been allotted the lands are by and large tilling it themselves. As the problem has not yet attracted the government's attention, there is no definite estimate of the numbers involved (Manas Dasgupta 16 July 1990, T.O.I., Baroda).

To rehabilitate the oustees of Tehri town which is being submerged by the Tehri dam, the government is building the new Tehri township. In the process, it is acquiring more land and consequently displacing other people. With limited land and so many claimants, resettlement seems to have become a game of musical chairs. Of course, the question that emerges is how long will even this land be enough for those who manage to get it?

Given that all projects cannot be halted, and with the increasing pressure on land, proportionately more and more persons are likely to be displaced involuntarily, either by the projects or because of the inability of the scarce resources to sustain them any longer. The Planning Commission (Seventh Five Year Plan 1985–90, Vol. 1) estimates that by the year 2000 the human population will be a little less than one billion and the animal population will also have increased considerably. The per capita availability of land, which was about 0.94 hectare in 1951, will decline to 0.33 hectare by the same year (Government of India, New Delhi 1985: 9).

Therefore, the best rehabilitation efforts notwithstanding, it is going to be increasingly difficult to accommodate all these people without displacing others. Life styles and occupational patterns might need to be changed. Just as fewer dams need to be constructed, along with other projects that exploit our natural resources, our dependence on these may have to be drastically reduced. We may have to learn to be more frugal in our consumption and ensure more efficient use of our existing resources.

Changes in occupational patterns will mean the acquisition of new skills, for which, as Dhagamwar says, the only solution is education. Even the oustees are beginning to realise that the scarce natural resources are not going to be able to sustain them, let alone future generations, for long. They will have to acquire new skills that would better equip them to face the future.

As we have seen, an examination of rehabilitation efforts indicate that they are more often than not *ad hoc* and project-specific. What is needed is a national policy according to which rehabilitation efforts can be undertaken with a degree of uniformity. Of course, there should be scope for variation to suit the cultural, social and geographical requirements of the local people.

The promises made have to be realistic and based on the actual availability of resources in order to avoid creating false hopes and aspirations. Demographic projections have to be made while preparing rehabilitation plans so that the increase in population during the gestation period of the project is accounted for.

Even with the very best of policies, the plight of the oustees will not improve unless these policies are implemented efficiently and adequately in advance. We have found that the authority responsible for rehabilitating the oustees was invariably the same as that implementing the project. The argument against this model is that since the main interest of the project authorities is in the speedy and successful implementation of the project, they cannot help but see the resettlement of the oustees as a secondary task and hence do not pay sufficient attention to it.

A separation of authority would help pin responsibility and encourage each department to do its work. But even this model does not seem to have succeeded. For example, land is acquired by the central government for the National Thermal Power Corporation (NTPC), for the construction of thermal power plants. The rehabilitation of the oustees, however, is the responsibility of the state in which the plant is to be located. The oustees of the Shaktinagar plant in the Singrauli area and the Talcher plant in Orissa have stories of inadequate and inappropriate resettlement to tell. They find themselves being pushed from one authority to the other, with each holding the other responsible. The oustees' ire is, however, directed against the NTPC, whom they regard as the establishment for whom their lands have been acquired.

Our experience has shown that until people organise themselves into a strong political lobby they will never be heard. The oustees of the Thalvayshet Fertiliser Project, or the villagers of Nhava Sheva whose lands were acquired to build the Jawahar Port, were able to organise themselves with the help of their leaders into a strong political lobby and have succeeded in getting reasonable compensation for their lands. In the current political scenario, no policy or law will be successful until the people themselves are in a position to compel the authorities to implement it.

Increasing the number of projects is not the solution, especially when the benefits accrue to only the priviledged few, while the others bear the costs. Our planning process has to ensure that along with an in-depth viability evaluation of the project taking into account all the social and environmental costs, there is an equitable distribution of benefits. Piecemeal plans and policies are not the solution. There is need for more holistic planning to enable better coordination between the various governmental bodies and departments.

At the same time, we must realise that we cannot continue with our present dependence on scarce natural resources. Only the most judicious use of these resources will ensure that there is enough to meet not only our needs but also those of future generations. It is time that we once again took heed of Mahatma Gandhi's warning 'The earth provides enough to satisfy every man's need, but not every man's greed.'

References

Anonymous. 1988. Of Forests and People. *Economic and Political Weekly.* 23 (25), Bombay.

Bhaskar Reddy, I. Uday. 1989. Costs of River Valley Projects in India. *Indian Journal of Public Administration.* 35 (3), July–September.

Cernea, Michael. 1990. *From Unused Social Knowledge to Policy Creation: The Case of Population Resettlement.* Development Discussion paper no. 342, Harvard Institute for International Development, USA.

Das Gupta, Manas. 1990. New Problems Dog Sardar Sarovar Project. *Times of India*, 26 July, Baroda.

Fernandes, Walter, J.C. Das and **Sam Rao.** 1989. *Displacement and Rehabilitation: An Estimate of Extent and Prospects.* In Walter Fernandes and Enakshi Ganguly Thukral, eds., *Development, Displacement and Rehabilitation.* New Delhi: Indian Social Institute.

Ganguly Thukral, Enakshi. 1989. *Dams for Whose Development?* In Walter Fernandes and Enakshi Ganguly Thukral, eds., *Development, Displacement and Rehabilitation,* New Delhi: Indian Social Institute.

Goldsmith, Edward and **Nicholas Hildyard.** *The Social and Environmental Effects of Large Dams,* Volume 2.

Karve, Iravati and **Jai Nimbkar.** 1969. *A Survey of People Displaced Through the Koyna Dam.* Pune: Deccan College.

Mankodi, Kashyap. 1989. *Displacement and Relocation: Problems and Prospects.* In Walter Fernandes and Enakshi Ganguly Thukral, eds., *Development, Displacement and Rehabilitation.* New Delhi: Indian Social Institute.

Multiple Action Research Group. 1991. *Sardar Sarovar Oustees in Madhya Pradesh What do they know?* Tehsil Kukshi, District Dhar.

National Centre for Human Settlement and Environment (NCHSE). 1986. *Documentation on Rehabilitation of Displaced Persons Due to Construction of Major Dams.* Vol. 1.

Narmada Control Authority. 1984. *Sardar Sarovar Project, Resettlement and Rehabilitation Programme.* Supplementary Report, October.

Paranjpye, Vijay. 1988. *Evaluating the Tehri Dam: An Extended Cost Benefit Appraisal.* New Delhi: Indian National Trust for Art and Cultural Heritage.

Roy, Dunu. 1985. *Politics of Environment in The State of India's Environment 1984–85, the Second Citizen's Report.* New Delhi: Centre for Science and Environment.

Government of India. 1985a. *Seventh Five Year Plan 1985–90.* Vol. 1. New Delhi: Planning Commission.

Government of India. 1985b. *Report of the Committee on Rehabilitation of Displaced Tribals due to Development Projects.* New Delhi: Ministry of Home Affairs.

2

The Hirakud Dam Oustees: Thirty Years After

PHILIP VIEGAS

The Hirakud Dam: Its Genesis

The Hirakud dam, the largest multipurpose river valley project in Orissa, is built on the river Mahanadi. Originating in the Raipur district of Madhya Pradesh, the Mahanadi flows south-east through the districts of Sambalpur, Dhenkanal and Cuttack into the Bay of Bengal. The main river has a length of 90 km but along its tributaries it has a total length of 853 km. With an average rainfall of 53.17 inches in the catchment area, the annual discharge of the river was estimated to be about one lakh cusecs. Between 1911 and 1937 floods were a regular feature. As a result, very little water was available for cultivation. The Hirakud dam was, therefore, conceived primarily as a flood control measure whereby the waters of the Mahanadi if stored could also be used for irrigation and power generation (Government of Orissa 1968: 10–11).

Note: I owe my gratitude to J.C. Das for his support during our discussions with the affected people of the Hirakud dam. I am also indebted to Shri Ramakanth Singh, Secretary, Gramasri and to Shri Mahatab, without whose unstinting support and assistance this project would not have been a successful and memorable one.

The story of the Hirakud dam goes back to the year 1937 when the renowned Indian engineer, M. Visvesaraya, suggested the construction of reservoirs as a flood control measure and insisted on investigating the feasibility of such a measure in the Mahanadi basin. The Flood Enquiry Committee in 1940, however, differed on this point and resisted from recommending such measures in view of the high cost of constructing large storage reservoirs. Rather, it suggested the construction of embankments on main rivers as an equally effective flood control measure. Further investigations in the Mahanadi basin were undertaken by the Central Water and Power Commission and in 1945, on the basis of its report, it was decided to construct a multipurpose storage dam on the Mahanadi which would not only check floods but also store sufficient water for irrigation and the generation of electricity. On these grounds the Commission suggested not one but three dams at three different points on the Mahanadi: Hirakud, Tikarpara and Naraj. However, only Hirakud was finally approved.

In March 1946, the foundation stone of the Hirakud dam was laid by the Governor of Orissa, Sir Harthrun Lewis. But the actual work on the dam commenced only in mid-1948. Being the first major river valley project of independent India, a second foundation was laid by the first Prime Minister of India on 12 April 1948.

The three major purposes of the Hirakud project were: (i) irrigation; (ii) power generation; and (iii) flood control. Although the purpose of this study is to look closely at those displaced by the project, it is important to take a quick look at the performance of the project as well.

Claims and Performance: The Schism Between

IRRIGATION

The main dam is 5 km in length and is the longest dam in the world. The concrete dam alone is 1.2 km long and the earthen dam 3.8 km. It has two dykes on either side of the earthen dam with a total length of 21 km. The reservoir formed by the dam is 743 sq km covering parts of Sambalpur and Raigarh districts. The maximum height of the masonry dam is 200 feet while that of the earthen dam is 195 feet, permitting a gross storage capacity of 6.6 million acre feet and at RL 590 their dead storage capacity is 1.88 million acre feet. The live storage capacity is 4.72 million acre feet.

The dam has two main canals, the Bargarh canal and the Sason canal, and a vast network of branch canals, distributaries, etc. Table 2.1 presents the details of the Hirakud dam canal network. With a total length of 3,373.83 km of canal network, the dam was expected to irrigate an area of 8 lakh acres with 100 per cent kharif intensity and 48 per cent rabi intensity (*Indian Express* 1987a: 8).

. Impressive though these statistics sound, the performance of the dam has been far from satisfactory. For instance, according to a paper presented by Dr Supakar at a seminar on Agricultural Production and Productivity in Orissa, of the envisaged 8 lakh acres only 3,83,907 acres have so far been brought under irrigation (*Indian Express* 1987a: 8). In other words, as far as irrigation is concerned, the dam operates effectively at 48 per cent of its originally envisaged capacity.

TABLE 2.1
The Hirakud Dam Canal Network

Sl. No.	Type of canal	Nos.	Length (in km)	Flow of water (in cusecs)
1.	Main canals	2	110.56	3,822 to 630
2.	Branch canals	2	35.12	902 to 506
3.	Distributaries	56	465.35	381 to 7
4.	Minor canals	85	306.78	43 to 1.3
5.	Sub-minor canals	23	45.38	43 to 1.3
6.	Sub-minors	3	6.16	43 to 1.3
7.	Water courses	2,056	2,404.48	Upto 1.0
	Total	2,227	3,373.83	

Source: Government of Orissa 1968: 18.

POWER

As regards power generation too, one observes a wide gulf between its installed capacity and actual performance. The dam has two hydroelectric plants with a total capacity of 270 MW. The actual generation, however, is restricted to 120 MW which is 44.4 per cent of the installed capacity. When questioned about the huge gap of 55.6 per cent between the installed capacity and the actual generation which, incidentally, is fed into the state power grid, a senior offical of the Hirakud hydroelectric unit told us that the gap is only an apparent one. According to him, the gap does not in fact exist because the two hydroelectric units of the dam are not expected to produce more than 120 MW of power at any given time and the surplus installed capacity is meant to compensate for a fall in the power supply to the state power grid. This means that the Hirakud Hydroelectric Power-station should not be seen as an isolated entity but as part of the entire state power system to which this unit is expected, on the one hand, to provide 120 MW at any given moment and, on the other, if necessary, increase its own supply so as to maintain the stable power supply of the state power grid when other power sources fail. Second, the surplus installed capacity of 150 MW of the two units is meant only as a stand-by in case of a failure of its other generating units. Although seemingly reasonable, these arguments still do not fully justify the significant gap between the installed capacity and its actual generation.

LIFE EXPECTANCY OF THE DAM

The life expectancy of the dam is yet another area that raises grave doubts about its performance. The expected lifespan of the dam is 100 years and, in fact, at the time of construction, it was expected to be more because of the provision of 64 deep sluice gates to carry the silt-laden monsoon water. These expectations, however, have been belied due to a high rate of siltation. The three cycles of hydrographic surveys conducted by the research team of the Hirakud Research Station, Hirakud, have shown a silt deposit of 6.6 ha m/100 sq km/year in 1979, 6.82 ha m/year in 1982 and 6.3 ha m/100 sq km/year in 1986, against an anticipated 2.5 ha m/100 sq km/year. In 1985, 29 years after the dam became operational, the total reduction in dead storage, live storage and gross storage capacity was 33.29 per cent, 12.62 per cent and 18.39 per cent, respectively. Table 2.2 presents the results of the studies on sedimentation in the Hirakud reservoir conducted by the research team of Hirakud Reservoir Research Station. These studies reveal that one-third of the dam is already practically useless.

A report in the *Indian Express* (1987a: 8) presenting the findings

TABLE 2.2
Loss of Storage Capacity of Hirakud Reservoir up to 1985

Storage	Cum.	New capacity	Siltation	Loss (in per cent)	Annual loss
Dead	2,262	1500.92	761.08	33.65	1.15
Live	5,843	5105.78	737.22	12.62	0.44
Gross	8,105	6614.70	1490.30	18.39	0.63

Source: Compiled from data provided by Hirakud Dam Research Station, Hirakud.

of the Orissa Remote Sensing Application Centre gives an even higher rate of siltation. It states that the reduction in the dead storage and total storage of the Hirakud dam till 1985 was 36.74 per cent, 14.01 per cent and 20.36 per cent, respectively. The annual loss is estimated to be 1.3 per cent of the dead storage, 0.5 per cent of the live storage and 0.7 per cent of the gross storage capacity. Although the figures in these two studies differ, it is more than evident that the rate of siltation is extremely high and is threatening the life of the dam. At the present rate of siltation (6.3 ha m/100 sq km/year), by the year 2056 AD when the dam will have completed 100 years, its gross storage capacity will be reduced by 63.4 per cent (Government of Orissa 1987). That is, in absolute terms, the dam's gross storage capacity will be reduced by 5138.57 cum. to 2,966.43 cum. from the original capacity of 8,105 cum.

The problem of siltation is further compounded by the total and indiscriminate denudation of the forest all around the Hirakud reservoir. Unparalleled deforestation has taken place between 1930 and 1975. In Sambalpur, 446.61 sq km, and around the neighbouring town of Jharsuguda, 453.01 sq km of forest area has been cut down (*Indian Express* 1987b: 8). Further, large-scale waterlogging and seepage around the dam has distinctly reduced the productivity of the land.

FLOOD CONTROL

Another major area where the dam seems to have belied expectations is that of flood control. One of the primary aims of the dam was to check floods which were a regular feature in the delta region. The situation, however, has not shown much improvement and floods continue to wreak havoc in the region. The worst floods were witnessed on 19 September 1980, described by *The Hindu* (20 September 1980: 1) as the 'highest ever floods'. Due to heavy rains in the Hirakud catchment area, the safety of the dam was at stake. Huge amounts of water, an estimated 12 lakh cusecs, had to be released on an emergency basis within a few hours. As a result, over one million people were affected by the gushing flood waters. Cuttack, Puri and Sambalpur districts were badly affected. This also caused flash floods in the Bansadhara river in Koraput district. Vast areas of Srikakulam district in Andhra Pradesh too were submerged without any prior warning. Over 144 villages were inundated. *The Hindu* (20 September 1980) reported that over 200 perished in the floods and there was no count of the cattle lost. Never before had Orissa experienced such catastrophe, thus raising serious doubts about the capacity of the dam to check floods. More recent reports about the development of cracks in the dam are causing grave concern to the entire population of Orissa.

Thus, in practically every field—irrigation, power generation or flood control—the dam has operated much below expectations. This is as far as the economics of the dam is concerned. The focus of this paper is, however, on the human dimension. It attempts to highlight the social costs incurred in the construction of the Hirakud dam, which are generally ignored in the cost-benefit analysis; and focuses, specifically, on the issues of land acquisition, compensation for land and houses, and on the government's rehabilitation scheme. While discussing these issues, particular emphasis is laid on the displaced persons and on the impact of displacement on their cultural, social and economic life.

Methodology

Field visits, discussions with the villagers, and interviews with significant individuals like leaders of village organisations, school teachers and the educated of the village constituted the major sources of our data. The selection of the villages was determined by the type of displacement caused and the kind of resettlement opted for by the displaced persons. Accordingly, to arrive at a more objective picture of the problems of land acquisition, compensation and rehabilitation, cluster sampling was done. Three clusters, defined on the basis of the following criteria, were identified:

1. Those villages that were only partially affected: These consisted of a set of villages wherein the inhabitants had lost only their cultivable land but not their houses.
2. Those villages that were fully affected: Here people had been totally displaced, losing both land and houses, but had rehabilitated themselves with no help from the government. They often settled themselves in already existing villages and were provided homestead land and in some cases even agricultural land by sympathetic villagers. For instance, some of the villagers of the erstwhile Sudda and Telgir villages in Sambalpur district migrated to neighbouring Surguja district in Madhya Pradesh, where they were provided rehabilitation by the Raja of Surguja.
3. Those villages that were fully displaced as in (2) but whose inhabitants were rehabilitated in camps set up by the Government.

The selection of these three clusters of villages and visits to the sites made possible first-hand information through discussions and direct observation. In all these villages, discussions were held mostly with the village elders, i.e., those 50 years old and above. This ensured that information was obtained only from those who had the direct experience of being uprooted by the construction of the dam and were therefore in the best position to provide accurate and reliable information on what really took place. Besides, information obtained in one village was checked and counterchecked in another for accuracy and reliability.

Further, the government officials directly involved in the rehabilitation of those displaced by the Hirakud dam and those presently entrusted with the job of land acquisition, compensation and rehabilitation were also interviewed. Some retired officials were thus included. These interviews were most enlightening and helped complete the picture. As a matter of fact, the various sources of information both rectified and complemented each other.

Acquisition of Land

The Government of Orissa set up the Hirakud Land Organisation Commission and entrusted to it the job of rehabilitating the oustees.

This Commission had three sub-sections under the direct charge of three Deputy Commissioners: for land acquisition, land reclamation and resettlement of the oustees. Each of these officers had clearly defined responsibilities with respect to his particular department, and all three were assisted by several junior officers.

Land for the Hirakud reservoir was acquired under the Land Acquisition Act, 1894. All land below RL 632 was acquired. Though no accurate figures on the extent of land acquired are available, according to one report, of the total 1,67,376.83 acres of submerged land, 1,15,127.97 acres was good agricultural land (Government of Orissa 1968: 13). Another source puts the total land lost at 1,82,592 acres, of which 1,23,000 acres was cultivable (Pattanaik, et al. undated: 13).

There is a similar variation in the number of villages submerged. Covering a vast area of 743 sq km, the Hirakud reservoir submerged 249 villages in Sambalpur district alone and in the adjoining Raigarh district of Madhya Pradesh, 36 villages were submerged (Government of Orissa 1968: 13). This figure, however, varies between 160 and 249. The more reliable figure seems to be that provided by a retired government official who was directly responsible for the resettlement of the oustees. He puts the figure of submerged villages at around 2,000. This, however, includes only the inhabited villages while the rest, according to him, were uninhabited villages. This also raises questions about the exact number of displaced persons. According to the Government of Orissa report (1968: 13), 22,144 families were affected, that is, a population of about 1.1 lakhs. The number of persons affected, however, varies between 1.1 and 1.6 lakhs. This lack of accurate data on as crucial an issue as this is itself an indication of both the central and the state governments' degree of concern for the rehabilitation of the oustees. Neither is there any precise data available regarding the tribal and non-tribal composition of the displaced persons. However, as the area is inhabited predominantly by Gonds, it may be assumed that a large proportion of those displaced were tribals belonging to this community.

Cash Compensation for Land

Land acquired from private landholders was compensated in cash payments. To enable a fair assessment of the land acquired, it was classified into 22 different types on the basis of productivity. The major categories were: *bahal* the most fertile low land; *berna* ranked next and was considered neither high nor low; *mal* was high land with slopes permitting a slow passage of water; *att* was high land depending mostly on the rains for its productivity; and *barcha* and *bari* were lands prepared with great labour near the village and irrigated by tanks or wells. Each of these was further subdivided into three or four categories based on quality. For instance, *bahal* lands were classified as *bahal abbal khari pani*, *bahal abbal pani*, *bahal madhyani*, and *bahal mamuli*.

Compensation was assessed on the basis of rental and market value. The former was calculated as 192 times the deduced rent of each class of land and the market value was calculated by sending officials to each area to assess the prevalent local price of land. On the basis of these the following rates were fixed and payment made to the land owners (Pattanaik, *et al*. undated: 15).

Bahal:	1)	Rs 600 to 1000 per acre
	2)	Rs 500 to 700 per acre
Berna:	1)	Rs 300 to 500 per acre
	2)	Rs 250 to 350 per acre
Mal:	1)	Rs 200 to 350 per acre
Atta:	1)	Rs 50 to 150 per acre
Barcha:	1)	Rs 400 to 600 per acre
Bari:	1)	Rs 300 to 400 per acre

Although the landowners were aware that the evaluation of the land was based on the criterion of the type or grade of land, they were still confused about the uniformity of the process of evaluation.

For instance, in the resettled village of Sharada we were told that grade 'A' land was valued at the rate of Rs 500 and grade 'D' land at the rate of Rs 200 per acre, while the value of the middle grade lands varied anywhere between these two extremes. As mentioned earlier, in addition to the extent of land, its quality too was an important factor in assessing its value. Most of this land was within the Mahanadi delta region and was thus very fertile for paddy cultivation. In fact, people testified to its fertility saying that land was so abundant and its productivity so high before the construction of the dam, that there was never any necessity to raise a second crop.

Given these conditions, however, the compensation paid raises questions about the basis of land assessment: in Luaboga village one person received Rs 25,000 for 32 acres, while the owner of a 26 acre plot got only Rs 7,000. Another owner of a 16 acre plot in the same village received only Rs 1,800. Of the two owners who had 13 acres each of the same grade of land, one was given Rs 4,000 and the other Rs 2,000. Another who had 6 acres was given Rs 1,045 while yet another person was paid Rs 450 for his 3 acres. Yet no explanations were offered by the authorities concerned.

People Ignored

Confronted with these discrepancies, the villagers were dumbfounded. Although some tried to find vague explanations, no one was able to say exactly how his land had been evaluated. This lack of knowledge is ironical in the light of the provisions in the law that require the government to clearly inform the people about the different aspects on which the evaluation and resettlement is based. On the contrary, the situation clearly indicates that, apart from informing them that their 'lands would be submerged', that 'they would have to evacuate' and 'they would be paid compensation', the Government took no pains whatsoever to make the villagers understand the crucial issues involved in the assessment of their land. At no point did the people feel that the government had taken them into confidence. They did, however, admit that the government officials had asked them how much compensation they would want for their land. But given their ignorance and naivete, the villagers threw away this opportunity and left it entirely to the 'benevolence' of the officials, saying, 'you know what is best; we trust you will give us what we deserve', little knowing that the officials would betray their trust. The cost of this was, of course, very great and they paid for it heavily.

Inadequate Compensation

Obviously the compensation was grossly inadequate. This is also evident from the fact that a handful of literates belonging to the upper class filed their cases in the High Court and some even pursued them to the Supreme Court and won a compensation of 300 to 400 per cent more than the original awarded to them by the government. In Luaboga village of Lakhanpur block in Sambalpur district, one farmer was given Rs 7,000 for 26 acres of good cultivable land. In the same village, another farmer was offered the same amount for 27 acres that also included a 2 acre orchard. But the latter, a farmer with a high social and economic status, refused to accept this unilateral decision of the government. He filed a petition in the High Court, pursued it to the Supreme Court where his appeal was upheld, and was awarded Rs 3 lakhs. In another instance, in Sharada village, a landholder took the initiative to take the government to Court and was awarded Rs 72,000 for his 10 acre plot.

Only those farmers who had legal documents to prove possession of lands were entitled to compensation. Those cultivators who had been cultivating land for several generations but had no legal documents to uphold their claim were categorised as landless. The eligibility for compensation for land was established on the basis of the Record of Rights (ROR) for each village which were prepared at the Hamir settlement in 1924. These records were supposedly updated from time to time and zonal officers were appointed at the time of land acquisition to check and update the existing land records. Yet, many in cultivating possession of lands continued to be without legal papers to prove possession. Naturally they were bitter that their rights of hereditary possession were totally ignored. A large number of cultivators were thus rendered landless and destitute as they received only a pittance as compensation for their houses.

Were the Record of Rights really updated to include the new lands that might have been acquired by a landholder during the period that lapsed between the preparation of the ROR and the acquisition of his land for the construction of the dam? This question is particularly pertinent in the case of the illiterate farmer and/or tribal farmer who, although aware that he had received compensation for his land, was unable to say whether he had been compensated only for a part of it or for all the land in his possession, that is, even for the portion of land that was acquired much after the preparation of the ROR but which might not have been recorded as such. This misgiving is not without basis in view of the fact that the provisions of the land acquisition scheme required zonal officers to visit each village and reside there until the land records had been corrected to the satisfaction of the people concerned. However, most of the displaced persons we met told us that the officers were seen in the village only when the land acquisition and evacuation notices were issued.

Cash compensation was also awarded for houses on the basis of the type: thatched, tiled (*pucca*), etc. As most of the houses were thatched, the compensation received by these was between Rs 100 and Rs 400. According to the displaced, in some areas, there was a rather unusual form of compensation. Aside from the usual distinction between a tiled and a thatched house, the owner was given compensation for the thatched house at the rate of Rs 100 per room. This was obviously to the advantage of the government, or rather the particular officials representing the government, because a typical rural house has no more than one or two rooms. Thus, the total compensation in most cases amounted to not more than Rs 100 or 200. Many owners of tiled houses alleged that their houses had been officially classified as thatched for the purpose of compensation. Thus, the process of disbursement was not only economically inadequate but also an utterly dehumanising experience.

Mode of Cash Disbursement

The disbursement of compensation took place within the village itself. The villagers were notified well in advance about the proposed date and plan for the distribution of compensation. On this day the Additional District Magistrate and the Tehsildar accompanied by other concerned officials and escorted by two armed policemen arrived in the village with the cash. The names of the recipients were announced, the cash was counted and distributed, after which the recipients' signatures or thumb impressions were taken. But the process was not quite so simple. Several unhealthy practices took place at this time according to the recipients. In some cases, as the cash was being given away, part of the compensation found its way into the pockets of the officials. This was vehemently maintained by the people and when questioned further one of them spoke out with a great deal of emotion: 'I have seen this. I am not making it up'. When asked why they did not protest, the recipients told us that they wanted to, but were intimidated by the two armed policemen who flanked the officials. With the memory still fresh in their minds, even 30 years later, the villagers reacted very strongly to this incident. They were still emotional but fear had given way to courage and self-respect. They said, 'Today if they [police] come even with guns, we will fight them with our bare hands'. It is strange and ironic that those very policemen who were there to guard against any pilferage and corruption and protect the rights of the poor turned out to be enemies in disguise,and protectors and guardians of the very evil they were supposed to guard against.

Money was siphoned off and the people were deceived in several other ways as well. For instance, the displaced persons were supposed to be provided free transport by the government. Yet people of the rehabilitation camps in Sangramal, Mura, Haldi and Katharbaga alleged that they were charged Rs 20 for this which was deducted from the compensation they received.

In Lachpalli village, the villagers claim that they were informed by the village heads, the *gauntia* and the *patwari*, that the entire village was allotted a total amount of Rs 4 lakhs in compensation for land, houses, trees, etc. However, the distributed money amounted to only Rs 2 lakhs and the remaining 50 per cent could not be accounted for!

Besides the deception and harassment that the displaced were forced to face, the process of cash disbursement itself was an extremely slow process. According to the schedule drawn up by the government, by March 1956 Rs 9.66 crores was to be disbursed as compensation to the oustees. By this date, however, only Rs 3.43 crores, that is, 35.5 per cent, had been officially distributed. Although over 64.5 per cent of the compensation had yet to be disbursed, by June 1956 everyone had been displaced (Pattanaik, *et al*. undated: 17). Even today many of the oustees have yet to receive their compensation, partial or full, and it is estimated that a few crores of the compensation money is still with the government.

Even the simple act of giving away the money of the recepients was turned into the most dehumanising experience with strong caste overtones. The officials seem to have found it too degrading to offer the money directly into the hands of recipients who belonged to the lower castes. Instead, they dropped it on to a sheet spread out on the ground. The recipient had to pick it up from the ground as a dog would the crumbs thrown at it. Is it surprising that the displaced persons remember this even after 30 long years?

Role of Local Leaders

Some of the affected persons complained that their own village *mukhiyas* too let them down. In one instance the *mukhiya* advised the villagers to surrender their lands without protest, assuring them that the government would take care of their needs. But when they needed him, the *mukhiya* had already left for Sambalpur and had settled there. In other areas the *mukhiyas* collected money in advance with promises of helping them. In the course of time, however, both the money and the *mukhiyas* disappeared.

In several cases the *mukhiyas* were won over by the government. They were awarded a handsome compensation for their land, so that once they were satisfied it was not difficult to keep the rest of the villagers quiet. Had they also been poorly compensated there would perhaps have been a stronger protest from the people. There was obviously an implicit understanding between the government and the local *gauntias*. Subsequently the people felt completely let down by the government as well as by their leaders. They still harbour strong feelings of resentment and it will perhaps be several generations before these deep-rooted emotions are erased.

Psycho-cultural Impact of an Alien Culture

Most of the villagers had very little contact with the outside world and were dazed spectators of the events that took place. Besides being illiterate, a significant number did not even know how to count and accepted what was given to them without question. They were even somewhat fascinated by the sight of so much money. As some of the recipients noted, it was the first time that they had handled such large sums of money. Although there was a deep sense of loss, there was also a certain degree of excitement. In this excitement and confusion it never occurred to the oustees, and particularly the tribals, that they ought to provide for their future and think in terms of long-term planning and management. In fact, they had never before had any reason to do so as they had always perceived the village as a self-sufficient unit and were accustomed to living from day to day. Thus, most of the villagers were totally at sea and easily misguided. Naturally, they fell prey to middlemen.

Petty businessmen too swooped down upon the villagers like hawks. Knowing they had money in hand, they invaded the area and turned the village into a virtual shopping centre overnight, with commodities like transistors, cycles, textiles, footwear and brassware to tempt the villagers. Liquor was available in abundance and gambling stalls were opened in defiance of the official law and order machinery, or perhaps in connivance with its 'upholders'.

This cultural invasion was just too overpowering for the oustees, especially the tribals, to handle. While earlier they had lost their houses and lands to the dam, now they had squandered practically their entire cash compensation and were reduced to a state of near destitution. All they were left with were a few colourful trinkets.

Protests, Agitations and the Government's Response

Not only did the Land Acquisition Act (1894) fail to provide for a full and fair compensation for land acquired, it also restricted it to the minimum and that too only to landowners with legal holdings. It also made no clear provisions permitting the landholder to raise objections about the amount of compensation paid. Nevertheless, objections were raised but these were dealt with as individual cases rather than as a community problem. Although all objections were of a similar nature, each individual had to present his/her case individually and each case was dealt with on the basis of its own merit.

The local officials were not empowered to deal with any such cases either. In most instances they ignored such complaints. In others, they merely told the villagers to file a writ petition in the High Court in Sambalpur, the district headquarters some 50 to 60 km away. For an illiterate villager, going to Sambalpur was too complex, expensive and even frightening. Moreover, such a step would only have added to his problems, increasing his vulnerability to exploitation at the hands of unscrupulous middlemen and lawyers. The distance, lack of adequate transport and other forms of communication between the village and Sambalpur were the other factors that discouraged anyone from pursuing his case in the High Court.

Those who did raise objections and filed petitions suffered for it as they were given only a part of the compensation as 'advance' on the grounds that the case was in Court and the balance would be paid only when the case was resolved. In some cases of this nature, officials offered to help and took away their compensation papers instead. By the time the people realised that they were being cheated it was too late, because by then both the officials and their papers had disappeared. Since without their documents they were unable to pursue their cases themselves, their protest resulted, not in better compensation, but in a loss of even the little they were entitled to.

It may be noted in this context that the normal procedure for lodging a complaint merely involved making a note of the objection in the official compensation document after receiving the full compensation. In other words, the law did not require that the complainant be given only partial compensation in order for his complaint to be legitimate but was entitled to his entire compensation regardless of the protest. All that he needed to do was merely state that he was accepting his compensation under protest. This regulation, however, was twisted and interpreted by the officials to suit their own sinister designs, on the basis of which they not only deprived them of their full compensation but also took away their valuable documents, even destroying the evidence required for obtaining the remaining part of their compensation.

Such were the tactics employed by the government to prevent any form of protest lest it result in a situation of total anarchy. Supporting this strategy was the rampant illiteracy, total ignorance and low social and economic status of the people. The petty officials turned the situation further to their advantage by effectively restricting the information communicated to the oustees to the minimum, thus ensuring only a muffled protest from them. In the final analysis, these tactics were so successful that they effectively curtailed even the most organised forms of protest.

The Protests of Sambalpur and Padampur

Even in the face of the government's efforts to muffle the voice of the people, there were a few attempts at organised protest in Sambalpur and Padampur towns under the banner of the Communist Party. Referring to these public protests, a Government of Orissa report states:

> The people had great doubts regarding the benefits in comparision to the present loss of their ancestral homes and best cultivated land. However, the agitation was curbed by elaborate propaganda regarding the agitation and the benefits of the dam and government took responsibility to provide all the people of the submerged area with land for cultivation and houses to live inside the district (1968: 11).

In Remta village, we had the opportunity to talk to the leaders who were involved in organising the Padampur protest meeting. These leaders were at the time President and Secretary of one of the several local *Yuvak Sangas* that were actively participating in the agitation. They told us that the people's demands at these public meetings were simple. They wanted full and proper compensation for their land, adequate rehabilitation of each village, and provision of basic facilities such as water, electricity, roads and schools. Violent clashes broke out between the agitating local people and the construction workers of the dam, most of whom were brought in from the south. The locals even allege that many of these workers had prior knowledge from their contractors of which lands were to be submerged. They bought a lot of land from the locals at a low price and later sold it at a huge profit. This precipitated the conflict between the locals and outsiders. Besides, the outsiders were obviously in favour of the dam as they not only had nothing to lose but only gained by way of employment and other unscrupulous activities. While the locals protested against the dam, shouting slogans such as *Hirakud bandh karo*, the outsiders too reacted using the same slogan but with a pun on the word *bandh*—to mean dam instead of *stop*. Such were the prevailing conditions that were primarily responsible for turning the protest meetings into violent agitations. The government seemed only too happy to take advantage of the situation and use it to justify the measures it took to curb the agitation. However, whether there was a clandestine and deliberate attempt to create friction between the two groups will always remain an open question. The government, therefore, lost no time in declaring the agitation illegal under Section 144, Cr.P.C. It arrested the leaders and dispersed the crowd with lathi charges.

By arresting the protest leaders the government achieved another important objective. It stopped communication between the people and their leaders, successfully preventing the dissemination of useful and relevant information. Lack of proper leadership and adequate information left the people entirely handicapped. Consequently, the movement lost its vigour and was eventually aborted.

Other Protests

There were minor protests at the micro level as well. But these were stemmed by sheer force. At the time of evacuation, for instance, the police lathi-charged the people and pushed them like cattle into overloaded trucks. An eye-witness testified to an incident where three people died falling from a truck in Kenapalli village. Similar incidents might have occurred elsewhere but he admitted frankly, 'about other villages, I don't know for sure'. In some cases, the people were driven far away and left in the middle of a thick forest.

Other eye-witnesses staunchly maintained that some villages, like Khajuridihi, were even set on fire but were not certain about who was responsible for it. Some said that it could have been the police whose sole aim was to force people out of their homes by any means available to them, without any regard, concern or respect for human life. Another respondent, a former school teacher, narrated an incident about a young woman in the last stage of pregnancy who was forced out of her house crudely and violently without regard for her condition. She gave birth to her child out in the open with nothing but a tree to provide shelter.

There is no doubt that the government was successful in effectively curbing the agitations. But did the government take its other responsibility of providing 'all the people of the submerged area with land for cultivation and houses to live' as seriously?

The Forgotten Victims of Development: Their Response

That the displaced have not in any way been the beneficiaries of the construction of the dam is quite clear from their reactions and present status 30 years later. They have only been its victims. Each one, without exception, emphatically maintained that while those on the other side of the dam are happy, 'we are suffering'. 'Our situation today is much worse than what it was before the dam' is a commonly heard refrain. Reduction to a state of near landlessness is an unmistakable sign of this. Where in the past each had an average holding of 15 to 20 acres of land, today they have no more than 1 to 3 acres. As a result, many have been reduced to the status of agricultural labourers from proud owner-cultivators. Referring to their submerged lands they said, most dejectedly, 'Earlier we were like lords with labourers working for us; but today we have been turned into labourers ourselves and find it degrading and even dehumanising to work under others.'

The mental and emotional strain underlying these expressions is more than evident and is an unmistakable pointer to the problem of psychological adjustment to a situation. For many it meant the adoption of an altogether new life style. Moreover, the extremely limited resources of the region put further restrictions on the alternatives available. It was, therefore, nothing less than a struggle for survival wherein the displaced persons accepted whatever came their way regardless of their preferences.

Coping with the new environment demanded, in many instances, the adoption of new occupations and the concomitant adjustment to a new socio-economic order and the adoption of a new life style. The loss of land affected many, thus imposing a new occupation on the rising number of landless. While in the past they had cultivated their own lands, they have today taken to agricultural labour, daily wage labour on construction sites and sale of firewood. Those for whom fishing was only a subsidiary occupation, cultivation being the primary occupation, have now taken up fishing as a means of livelihood in the absence of other alternatives. Urda-Jharapara is one such village. The socio-economic status of this village is extremely low and the villagers live practically like outcastes on an island. Even a portion of the draw-down land is not available to them. It has all been distributed among the neighbouring villagers who are also those ousted by the Hirakud dam. Similarly, the Meher caste, traditionally weavers of Sambalpuri cloth as also cultivators, have taken to weaving exclusively as a result of losing land, thus reducing their income considerably. According to a rough estimate calculated on the basis of labour input and wages offered by the cooperatives, each weaver earns on average just about Rs 3 per day. There are several other features and dimensions to this issue, all pointing to a highly exploitative system. The fishermen's cooperative society is one example. The executive members of these societies, for instance, are outsiders who take advantage of the situation and resort to unscrupulous deception of the ignorant and illiterate village society members. But these are issues that need to be discussed at greater length on another occasion. Suffice it to point out here that the exploitative nature in the genesis and functioning of these societies may be traced back to the construction of the Hirakud dam. Prior to the dam the business of fishing and weaving was highly localised and the marketing system very simple. After construction began, the situation became too complex for the illiterate tribals and villagers to comprehend with the result that they became increasingly vulnerable to exploitation.

Many others who lost their lands bought some land in the resettled villages with part of the compensation money. In some villages the oustees acquired the village *gochar* (grazing) lands, and distributed it among themselves. In villages like Kadamdihi, a sympathetic *gauntia* seeing the plight of his co-villagers offered them his own land nearby and invited them to resettle there. A similar instance is narrated of the Raja of Surguja in Madhya Pradesh, who too offered the oustees land for housing and cultivation. Thus, all those who managed to acquire a piece of land took to cultivation.

Several families migrated to other states like Madhya Pradesh, Uttar Pradesh and Rajasthan where they had relatives, in the hope that they would get some sympathetic support from them. Others were separated from their families in the hope of finding a job in the unorganised tertiary sector. And those who decided to remain had to resign themselves to the situation and make the best of the worst.

These are only some of the salient features of the adjustment process. A deeper study that will throw light on the more specific psychological strain and stress experienced by the displaced persons is an urgent necessity.

The Rehabilitation Camps

It has already been mentioned that the government had organised camps to rehabilitate those displaced by the Hirakud dam. This involved clearing up vast areas of rich natural reserve forest, reclaiming the land for cultivation and providing transport to enable the people to settle down in the newly-developed camps. These camps were located at a distance of 50 to 60 km from their original habitations but were within Sambalpur district itself. It was communicated to all the oustees that the government would be setting up such camps and that the people were free to avail themselves of this facility.

Most, however, did not accept the government's scheme and preferred to find their own alternative. It is estimated that not more than 11 per cent resettled in these camps (Pattanaik *et al.* undated: 55). The reasons for this are varied. Some felt that the camps were too far from their original village. Others had no faith in the government's scheme and found the uncertainty of a new location and environment too overwhelming. Still others took advantage of the hospitality of a neighbouring village and opted to settle there. Besides, since no transport was provided to shift their cattle and housing materials such as tiles, bricks and wood, some found it much more convenient to shift to a nearby locality where they could make use of the old materials to construct their new houses. Also, it was easier to walk their cattle to a nearby location than to take them to the camps 50 km away.

Those who did go to the rehabilitation camps found to their chagrin that there was nothing but a cleared land area. They had to make a new beginning, starting with the construction of their houses for which they incurred further losses because they needed new housing materials. Having constructed the house the next step was to obtain cultivable land. The vast forest area that had been cleared was made available to them at the rate of Rs 225 to 425 per acre. Those who could afford it bought the land but were allowed no more than 3.5 acres per person although they had earlier been promised 5 acres.

We had the occasion to visit two camps, Sangramal A and B, situated about 35 km from Sambalpur town. The camps are approached from the main road via Parmanpur village and lie about 10 km from the main road. Each of these camps is composed of five village settlements consisting of about 200 households each. The total population in these two camps is about 10,000. The camp is provided with a post-office, a primary health centre and a lower primary school. Over the last few years, however, the villagers have managed to upgrade the high school land. The percentage of literates in the camp is fairly high, around 80 to 85 per cent. This camp has also been provided with a community centre, built at a cost of Rs 85,000 in 1956. Facing this is a temple which was built in 1975 by the villagers themselves. Triumphantly, but with a mixture of cynicism, they pointed out the temple, an architecturally and aesthetically fine structure, and said that it cost them Rs 23,000 in 1975. The underlying message being that the community centre, a rather crude structure built by the government, should not have cost more than Rs 10,000 in 1956. Drinking water is also available here. A dug-well was provided initially but they now have four tube-wells. For irrigation the government has provided six *khattas* (ponds), of which today five are functional. However, because of their insufficient depth, they are able to provide irrigation water only for the kharif season. Canals too were built but are, for all practical purposes, dysfunctional.

In many cases the people alleged that the reclamation of land was haphazard. For instance, although the forest was cleared the tree stumps were not uprooted, making cultivation impossible. Instead of levelling the land with mud, ditches were filled up with branches and then covered with some mud to give a semblance of levelling. This was of course washed away during the first rains.

Although there was a separate body constituted by the government to look after reclamation of the land, lack of a proper monitoring system rendered the implementation of the scheme a virtual failure.

However, the overall impression from a visit to these camps is that these villagers are comparatively better off than those who refused to settle in these camps. This is also corroborated by the villagers themselves. Yet there exists an unmistakable and pervading sense of misery for their plight and nostalgia for the past. As one of them put it, 'If that [past] is 16 annas this [present condition] is only 5 annas.' And another, with a dejected expression added, 'You can look at our faces and tell.' He was right. Still writ large on their faces was a deep and lingering sense of pain and loss.

Conclusion

The primary reason for the failure of the government's rehabilitation effort seems to lie in the fact that it failed to percieve the issue of displacement in its totality and looked at it merely from an economic point of view. Hence, the alternatives it offered were exclusively of an economic nature with a total absence of the human dimension. Land was acquired from the people, compensation paid, and a rehabilitation scheme drawn up. But in all this, those directly affected were ignored and not consulted. There was a total lack of people's involvement and participation and at no stage were they taken into confidence. All decisions regarding them were taken unilaterally by the government. These decisions were merely communicated to the people and worse, imposed upon them. Nor was any attempt made, opportunity created or body constituted to appreciate the concerns and needs of the affected people.

The compensation itself was extremely inadequate and the rehabilitation scheme lacked an integrated approach. The problem was further compounded by the unhealthy practices adopted by both government officials, petty businessmen and middlemen. This further added to the stress and strain of displacement. The presence of widespread corruption and exploitation demands that, in addition to drawing up a scheme and appointing an implementing agency, the government should see that the scheme is carried out fully and the displaced persons are settled satisfactorily. In-built regular checks and monitoring measures would have restricted corrupt practices to the minimum.

Another significant issue emerges from the high rate of illiteracy among the affected people and their low exposure to outside culture. The semi-urban culture which suddenly burst upon their tradition-bound society, created a culture shock which the people in general and the tribals in particular were unable to comprehend and resolve. That the people should be able to succesfully encounter such a shock wave is either not even thought of or is simply presumed. Therefore, to equip the villagers to succesfully handle their new socio-economic environment caused by the onslaught of an alien culture, the affected people need to be educated and mentally prepared. As has emerged from our discussion, most of the dispossessed unwittingly fell victim to this shock wave. They squandered all the money they had received as compensation and were reduced to a state of near destitution. Had they been prepared in advance for this, perhaps the shock would not have had such a devastating effect.

Finally, while a developmental infrastructure along with its concomitant problems of displacement etc. is a necessary evil that cannot be done away with, the pain and human suffering that is generated in its wake can to a large extent be cushioned. In this context, to the extent feasible, the oustees might have been permitted and even encouraged to find their own alternatives for resettlement and should have been supported in their effort. Coercing them to resettle in artificially created rehabilitation camps can only serve to aggravate the pain of resettlement. Had, for instance, the Hirakud oustees who made a heroic attempt to settle down in areas of their choice received some financial and other support from the government by way of provision of public facilities like drinking water, schools, PHCs, etc., they would have long forgotten their hurt and loss and would have rehabilitated themselves within a short period. On the contrary, even today, the Revenue Department refuses to recognise those villages in which the displaced persons have rehabilitated themselves. Tilgi and Urda are two examples. As a result, these villages fall outside the existing administrative structure and are not under the purview of any development schemes.

The first Prime Minister of India, Pandit Jawaharlal Nehru, in his speech at the foundation laying ceremony told the villagers, 'If you are to suffer, you should suffer in the interest of the country' (*The Bombay Chronicle* 12 April 1948: 5). The people did exactly that. But does the country even recognise this suffering and is it doing something to soften that pain? Or is the country victimising these people in the interest of a few? In fact, the prevailing sentiment among the oustees even 30 years later is well expressed by the villagers of Lachpalli: 'The government has got whatever it wanted of us, but we have not received anything from it.'

References

Government of Orissa. 1968. *Report on the Benefits of Hirakud Irrigation: A Socio-Economic Study*. Cuttack: Bureau of Statistics and Economics.

Government of Orissa. 1987. *Third Report—1986, Sedimentation Studies in Hirakud Reservoir*. Hirakud: Irrigation and Power Department, Hirakud Dam Research Station.

Indian Express. 1987a. Hirakud Dam Defects Pointed Out, 21 July.

Indian Express. 1987b. Hirakud Dam Fast Silting up. 25 August.

Pattanaik, S.K., B. Das and **A. Mishra**. Undated. Hirakud Dam Project: Expectations and Realities. In Participatory Research in Asia, *People and Dams*. New Delhi.

3

Whatever Happened to Muddavat Chenna? The Tale of Nagarjunasagar

MRIDULA SINGH •
RANJAN KUMAR SAMANTRAY

Muddavat Chenna is a migrant labourer, one of the 28,000 people displaced by the Nagarjunasagar dam in Andhra Pradesh. In 1962, Muddavat, along with 50 families from submerged village Guvvala-gutta, was given a house plot in Mutkur. The 5 acre holdings given to these families were 25 to 30 kms away in Mursapenta hamlet of Kandlagunta. The distance between the houses and their lands obviously made it difficult for the new occupants to protect their lands from encroachment by the local population. For six years they continuously pursued the matter with the *tehsildar* of Macherla and the Collector of Guntur. The ousted families spent their compensation amount running from one office to the other without being able to retrieve their encroached lands. Muddavat

Note: We were assisted in this study by Mr Venkat Reddy a member of AWARE, a NGO based in Hyderabad. He proved invaluable as both a guide and translator during our field visits. We also owe our gratitude to Mr. P.K.S. Madhavan, Chairman AWARE, Mr K.P.S. Prasad, Dy. Supt. Engg., Mr. R. Satya Narayan Rao, Documentation Officer of the Bureau of Economics and Studies, Mr. Dharma Rao, Executive Engineer and Mr K. Nageshwar Rao. Dy. Supt. Engg. for their help and cooperation in making this study possible.

Chenna and the other 50 families soon joined the vast category of landless labourers and now work for daily wages.

Muddavat Chenna is only a case in point. Studies on rehabilitation have revealed that displacement not only creates psychological and cultural insecurity but also takes away the existing livelihood of the oustees without offering any viable means of sustenance. Muddavat is one among approximately 5,098 families who were displaced by the Nagarjunasagar project (NSP). Although his is perhaps one of the worst experiences of displacement and rehabilitation due to the project, the condition of the others is not very different. Though the objective of this study is to focus primarily on the conditions of the affected population, Muddavat Chenna for instance, it is also important to look into the purpose of the project itself.

The Nagarjunasagar is a multipurpose river valley project in the valley of Nagarjunakonda in Andhra Pradesh, about 166 km southeast of Hyderabad, and is built across the river Krishna which rises in the Western Ghats near Mahabaleshwar. After flowing 1,400 kms through Maharashtra, Karnataka and Andhra Pradesh, it falls into the Bay of Bengal. Its drainage area is 2,58,948 sq kms, of which 26.8 per cent lies in Maharashtra, 43.8 per cent in Karnataka and 29.4 pcr cent in Andhra Pradesh.

The river Tungabhadra joins the Krishna at Songameswaram in Andhra Pradesh. The distance between the confluence and the Nagarjuna dam site is 130 km. It is within this range that the two large reservoirs of Srisailam and Nagarjunasagar are located.

Historical Background of the Valley

The Nagarjunakonda valley is well-known for its rich archaeological relics, many of which were tragically submerged due to the Nagarjunasagar reservoir. The project takes its name from the Buddhist philosopher of the 2nd century AD, Nagarjuna.

In fact, Nagarjunakonda provides an important landmark in the history of Buddhist architecture in India. During the rule of the Ikshvaku, in the latter period of the 3rd century AD, the valley boasted magnificent Brahmanical and Buddhist structures.

Before the submergence, efforts were made to salvage these

ruins. The excavation exposed more than a hundred sites from some dating back to the early stone age to some as late as the latter part of the medieval period. All these monuments were reconstructed at Nagarjunakonda.

The effort put in to replicate the monuments is commendable provided similar efforts were made to rehabilitate the oustees, which was not the case as far as Muddavat and many others were concerned.

The Project

According to the socio-economic survey conducted by Andhra University, the average rainfall in the command area before the project commenced was 35 inches (Nagabhushanam and Rao 1969: 37). The command area of the NSP lies on both banks. It is primarily a red soil area with patches of black soil, a soil type that favours wet-cropping. Given the cropping pattern and the low rainfall, the area faced an acute scarcity of water.

Although there were quite a few rain storage tanks on both sides of the command area, the volume of water preserved in these tanks was not at all sufficient for wet-cropping. The common factor that existed on both banks was scarcity of water for irrigation which constituted the prime reason for the construction of the NSP. The project was initiated in 1955 but construction began two years later in 1957. It was completed by 1969, except for the erection of the spillway gates, which was completed in 1973–74. The dam comprises two canals. The one on the left of the dam is called Jawaharlal Canal and the one on the right, Lal Bahadur Canal. The construction work on both canals started in 1956 and water was first released on 4 August 1967.

Salient Features of the NSP

   Hydrology
   Maximum flood discharge

Estimated	10,88,500 cusecs
Observed	10,60,880 cusecs
Watershed area at dam site	83,087 sq miles
Mean annual run-off at dam site	1,496 TMC

Maximum annual rainfall in the catchment	889 mm (35 inches)

Reservoir

Maximum reservoir elevation	594 feet
Storage capacity at 590 RL	9.33 maf
Waterspread area at 590 RL	110 sq miles
Dead storage level	489 feet
Dead storage capacity	3.86 maf
Live storage	5.47 maf
Total length of Masonry dam	4,756 feet
Length of left earthen dam	8,400 feet
Length of right earthen dam	2,800 feet

The Canals

Jawaharlal Canal (left canal)	295 km
Lal Bahadur Canal (right canal)	202.80 km

ECONOMICS OF THE PROJECT

The project was submitted to the Central Water Commission in March 1954 at an estimated cost of Rs 91.12 crores which was approved by the Planning Commission in September 1960. The first revised estimate of Rs 163.54 crores was approved by the Planning Commission in June 1969. The latest esimated cost available from the Status Reports of the NSP (Government of Andhra Pradesh 1989) was Rs 683.75 crores till the end of the Seventh Five Year Plan.

The cost of the project was met by the budget allocated under each Plan (see Table 3.1) and by a loan from the World Bank.

The loan from the World Bank was sought in 1975–76 and was necessary to meet the escalated costs. The World Bank appraised the project in 1976, estimated the balance cost of the project at Rs 267.30 crores, and sanctioned a loan of Rs 130.50 crores in the same year. This loan was not only to complete the balance work but also for the construction of ayacut roads, land development, etc.

IRRIGATION POTENTIAL OF NSP

Though the NSP was designed as a multipurpose project, the primary objective of this dam was to irrigate 11.05 lakh hectares of semi-arid land in seven districts of Andhra Pradesh. According to

TABLE 3.1
Plan-wise Expenditure from Commencement

Plan	Year	Expenditure (Rupees in lakhs)
1st Five Year Plan	1955–60	2,917.63
2nd Five Year Plan	1960–65	5,499.02
3rd Five Year Plan	1965–70	7,392.84
4th Five Year Plan	1970–75	4,025.72
5th Five Year Plan	1975–80	16,168.21
6th Five Year Plan	1980–85	18,470.09
7th Five Year Plan	1985–88	6,157.22
Total		60,630.73

Source: Government of Andhra Pradesh 1989: 11.

the Status Report of the NSP (Government of Andhra Pradesh 1989), Satennapalle, Vinukonda, Narsaraopet, Guntur, Batala and Ongole *talukas* of Guntur district and Makarpur *taluka* of Kurnool district had been covered under the right canal by 1986. Mirialguda and Hazurnagar *talukas* of Nalgonda district, Khammam *taluka* of Khammam district, and Nandigama *taluka* of Krishna district were covered by the left canal. Nellore district on the right side and Godavari district on the left had still to receive water in 1986. Thus, even two decades after the completion of the project, the target of seven districts has not been achieved. Only five districts have received irrigation.

ENERGY

The project plans proposed that energy would be generated under three heads:

1. Main dam site units
2. Right canal units
3. Left canal units

There are eight units at the dam site, one with a capacity of 110 MW and seven units of 100 MW each. The right canal head sluices were provided with three un:ts with a capacity of 30 MW each, and under the left canal it was proposed that there would be three units of 30 MW each. But according to the Status Report (Government of Andhra Pradesh 1989), the three units of the left canal were still under construction.

THE EXPECTED AND ACTUAL IRRIGATION POTENTIAL

The project was estimated to provide irrigation to 11.05 lakh hectares of parched land. The actual irrigation provided till July 1986 was 7.87 lakh hectares (Government of Andhra Pradesh 1989). Thus, 17 years after the project was completed, only 73 per cent of the target has been met. The Status Report (ibid.) cites various reasons for this.

1. The seepage losses contemplated at the time the project was formulated were 2 cusecs M.sft in the lined and 6 cusecs per M.sft in the unlined sections respectively. In reality, the losses were found to be 24 cusecs per M.sft in the main lined canal and 14 cusecs per M.sft in the unlined branch canals.
2. According to K. Nageswar Reddy, Executive Engineer of the NSP, some restrictions were imposed on the farmers in the command area for the distribution of water. They were to allocate only one-third of their land to wet crops and two-thirds to dry crops. However, the unauthorised conversion of two-thirds to wet crops and one-third to dry crops by some farmers led to scarcity of water in tail end areas.[1]
3. There was unauthorised cultivation outside the localised[2] area.
4. Indiscipline among the farmers who indulged in cross-bunding of canals and widening of banks and tampered with the regulating structure has also resulted in heavy wastage of water.

Cropping Pattern

The project was designed to provide irrigation to the dry agricultural lands of Andhra and Telengana regions of Andhra Pradesh. The irrigation facilities substantially improved cropping intensity and crop yield (Table 3.2), but had no overall impact on the cropping pattern.

Table 3.2 shows clearly that the yields of all crops except jowar and pulses have substantially increased. While the yield of jowar

---

[1] This was disclosed to the MARG team by K.Nageswar Reddy during an informal discussion on 24 April 1989.

[2] Localised: pocket of command area.

TABLE 3.2
Yields of Principal Crops

| Crop | Normal Yield Tonnes/Hectare (1984–87) | | |
	Command	Non-command	Difference (per cent)
1. Rice	2.45	2.11	16.1
2. Jowar	1.00	1.00	Nil
3. Pulses	0.50	0.70	29.6
4. Ground-nut	1.42	0.86	65.1
5. Chillie	2.80	2.50	12.0

Source: Subramanyam et al. 1989.

remained the same, there was a decline in the output of pulses from 0.70 tonnes per hectare to 0.50 tonnes per hectare.

There is a difference between the cropping patterns on the left and right canals. On the left, paddy accounts for 45 per cent of the irrigated area, chillie for 22 per cent, ground-nut for 13.6 per cent, cotton for 6.8 per cent and other dry crops for 12.6 per cent. The ratio of irrigated wet (IW) and irrigated dry (ID) is 1:1.2. On the right, paddy is the only wet crop and occupies 25 per cent of the irrigated area. The ratio of irrigated wet and irrigated dry is 1:3.

Submergence

The reservoir, covering an area of 110 sq miles, stretches from Mirialguda and Devarkonda talukas of Nalgonda district and Achampet taluka of Mahboobnagar district on the left bank to Paland taluka of Guntur district on the right bank. According to the dam site office, it has submerged 29,506 acres of agricultural land, 1,078 acres of government land, and 147 acres of house plots and structures. Data on forest land submerged was not available. A total of 26 villages and 31 hamlets were submerged. Data on the number of families displaced by the project is found to be varying. According to a government memo on rehabilitation dated 19 January 1960 a total of 1,500 families would be displaced. According to the Status Report (Government of Andhra Pradesh 1989: 8), 4,830 families were displaced. Unofficial figures (G.Lakshmi n.d.) show that 5,098 families were displaced, a total population of

28,000. Though the work at the dam site began in 1955 and displacement in 1959, the concerned government departments were not aware of the total number affected even in 1960. It is evident then that the affected population was given scant consideration when the dam was initiated.

Rehabilitation Sites

According to the Status Report (Government of Andhra Pradesh 1989: 8), 42,797.47 acres of land was allotted for rehabilitation. Of this, 41,241.96 acres were given by the forest department. The Report also mentions that the oustees had been rehabilitated in 24 main centres and 11 subsidiary centres. Of these, eight main and two subsidiary centres are on the right side of the river in the Macherla *taluka* of Guntur district, and 16 main centres and nine subsidiary centres are on the left side of the river in Mirialguda, Devarkonda and Bhungiri *talukas* of Nalgonda district. The Report does not mention the names of these centres or their location. No official lists with these details were available at any of the offices concerned. All that was available was a map at the site office indicating 23 main centres. The 11 subsidiary centres were not indicated and none of the officials seemed to know where these subsidiary centres were. Our team was told that as the rehabilitation was completed by the mid-1960s, the office had since ceased to exist. Nobody knew where the documents might have been removed to from the dam site office.

Out of 23 centres, five are in Macherla *taluka*, six in Devarkonda *taluka*, one in Bhungiri and 11 in Mirialguda *taluka*. Our team selected 13 centres from Mirialguda, Devarkonda and Macherla *talukas*, based on a random sample. None of the subsidiary centres could be included for lack of available information.

One centre from Bhungiri *taluka* was also not included as it was at a great distance from the other three *talukas*.

Our team was unable to visit two centres, Pogulla and Rekula-gadda from Devarkonda *taluka*, as they were inaccessible. One centre, Wazerabad in Mirialguda *taluka*, was found to be abandoned. Our team thus visited 10 centres—Rekkuraram Tanda and Kothapullareddipuram in Macherla *taluka*, Gandhi Nagar, Rajagutta, Shanti Nagar, Prem Nagar and Kothanandikonda in

Mirialguda *taluka*, and Kambalapalli, Usmankunta Tanda and Teldevalapalli in Devarkonda *taluka*.

We found that in fact the oustees were not rehabilitated in most of the main centres indicated on the map. Instead. they were resettled in hamlets situated 10 to 15 km away from the main centres, with different names from those mentioned in the official map (Table 3.3).

TABLE 3.3
List of the Main Rehabilitation Centres

The government list 1	Our findings 2	Taluka 3	District 4
1. Lachammbavi	Rekkuraram Tanda H/o (Hamlet of) Lachhambavi	Macherla	Guntur
2. Kandlagunta	Kothapullareddipuram H/o Kandlagunta	Macherla	Guntur
3. Dilwarpur	Gandhi Nagar H/o Dilwarpur	Mirialguda	Nalgonda
4. Rajagutta	Gandhi Nagar	Mirialguda	Nalgonda
5. Kallepalli	Shanti Nagar H/o Kallepalli	Mirialguda	Nalgonda
6. Chintapalli	Prem Nagar H/o Chintapalli	Mirialguda	Nalgonda
7. Kothanandikonda	Kothanandikonda H/o Mulkacherla	Mirialguda	Nalgonda
8. Kambalapally	Kambalapally	Devarkonda	Nalgonda
9. Yalmalamanda	Usmankunta Tanda H/o Yalmalamanda	Devarkonda	Nalgonda
10. Teldevalapalli	Teldevarapalli	Devarkonda	Nalgonda
11. Wazerabad	Wazerabad	Mirialguda	Nalgonda
12. Pogulla	Pogulla	Devarkonda	Nalgonda
13. Rekulagadda	Rekulagadda	Devarkonda	Nalgonda
14. Chitriyal	Not visited	Devarkonda	Nalgonda
15. Peddagutta	Not visited	Mirialguda	Nalgonda
16. Yallapur	Not visited	Mirialguda	Nalgonda
17. Dongapaddu	Not visited	Mirialguda	Nalgonda
18. Gurrambodu	Not visited	Mirialguda	Nalgonda
19. Venkatapur	Not visited	Bhungiri	Nalgonda
20. Tummarakota	Not visited	Macherla	Guntur
21. Mutukur	Not visited	Macherla	Guntur
22. Guttikonda (abandoned)	Not visited	Macherla	Guntur
23. Mulakacherla	Not visited	Macherla	Guntur

Source: Nagarjunasagar Dam Site Office and MARG survey.

Brief Profile of the Oustees

Our team visited 10 centres where approximately 2,277 of the 5,098 displaced families (45 per cent) are rehabilitated. As mentioned earlier, these families moved here only after being displaced. Most of the villagers opted to be resettled as a unit, in one centre. In some cases, the villagers were divided into smaller units and resettled at the new site with oustees from another submerged village, because they had little time to exercise their choice.

The oustees informed us that approximately 36 per cent of the population belong to the scheduled tribes, most of them to the Lambada tribe. About 7 per cent of the oustees from these 10 centres belong to the scheduled castes. The 45 per cent belonging to Other Backward Classes include Mangali Gauds, Golas, Mutrasis, Erkalis, etc. The remaining 12 per cent are from other caste groups, the Reddys for instance. As in other such projects, in this case as well, it is the socially and economically weaker sections of society that comprise the majority of the displaced. In most of the centres, people from various castes and tribes had been resettled together by the government and there were no caste-wise settlements in evidence, as is usually the case in rural India.

In Teldevalapalli, however, our team encountered a strong divide between the Reddys on the one hand, and the rest, i.e., the Lambadas and the Scheduled Castes, on the other. In fact, the two groups lived in separate settlements. When we met the Reddys and mentioned that we would be holding a meeting with the 'others', one of the men asked, 'why do you need to meet them, what do they know?'

The oustees lived in mud *kuccha* houses with thatched roofs which they had constructed themselves. The fields were located close to the settlements. According to the oustees, almost 60 to 65 per cent of the families, prior to displacement, owned on average 10 to 15 acres of land. Others had been tilling lands they had encroached upon. The landless were either engaged in sharecropping or worked as agricultural labour.

Our team found that even though the area submerged was vast, the population displaced was relatively small. In other words, the area was sparsely populated. However, many of those who had held land before displacement found that they were unable to sustain themselves on the small holdings allotted to them and were forced to migrate in search of daily wages.

Process of Displacement

LEVEL OF INFORMATION AT THE TIME OF DISPLACEMENT

The oustees told us that in 1955 the foundation stone of the dam was laid by the late Prime Minister, Pandit Jawharlal Nehru, and that they had attended the ceremony.

Kanka Reddy from Teldevalapalli said, 'Nehru in his speech had mentioned that Rs 370 crores will be spent and 20 villages will be submerged but many people will benefit from this dam.'

Bhramaya from Prem Nagar said, 'before the foundation stone was laid the government built colonies on the right and left banks of the river and the government officials came to survey the area. They told the villagers that a dam will be constructed.' Chennaya from Kothanandikonda said, 'before Nehru came, bulldozers were brought to level the land and construct roads. The officials tolds us that a dam will be built.'

Apart from what they heard in Nehru's speech, the people had very little information about the extent of submergence. Though some officials had mentioned the dam, they told the villagers little else at the time. However, once the process of land acquisition began, information began to filter down to the people.

ACQUISITION OF LAND

As mentioned earlier, the construction of the dam began in 1955, but the initial survey of the individual holdings to be acquired began in 1957.

The socio-economic survey was conducted in the submerged villages as the time of displacement approached. Those resettled in Kothapullareddipuram centre told us that their submerged village was surveyed in 1957, and those at Shanti Nagar and Kothanandi-konda centres said that their villages had been surveyed in 1958. The people now resettled in Teldevalapalli, Kambalapalli, Rek-kuraram Tanda, Rajagutta, Gandhi Nagar, Prem Nagar and Usmankunta Tanda centres told us that their villages were surveyed between 1961 and 1965. The surveys were conducted by the *tehsildar* and the Revenue Inspector who measured and filled in the details about the houses themselves. The detailed information regarding landholdings was collected directly from the Revenue Office without consulting the oustees. No information from the oustees was sought by the surveyors regarding the trees and wells on their lands.

Under the Land Acquisition Act, a public notice under Section 4 and a public declaration under Section 6 have to be issued before the issue of individual notices for final acquisition under Section 9. None of the oustees were aware of any notice under Section 4 or declaration under Section 6. This could be because they were illiterate and therefore the written medium of communication was meaningless to them.

The oustees received the notice under Section 9 which indicated the individual holdings to be acquired. These notices were issued to individuals by the *tehsildar* and the *patwari*. They held village meetings and explained the details before handing the oustees their notices.

DISPLACEMENT

Although the oustees had been told about their impending displacement, both by the officials concerned and by the local leaders, they were unable to accept the fact that the dam might result in their lands being submerged and their being displaced. Even if the waters did rise, they thought, it would not reach their village because it was at a level higher than the river.

The oustees resettled at Rekkuraram told us that the local MLA, G. Narain Reddy, held meetings every 15 days to explain the details about the displacement and rehabilitation policy. Budda said, 'the MLA promised us that we will get land and house plots and civic facilities.' Rammani said, 'though we were informed about our displacement, we thought that it would never happen during our life time.'

As a result, the people made little or no effort to identify alternative sites. When the waters finally began to rise and submergence and displacement became an irrevocable reality, some oustees moved up to higher slopes while others had to be forcibly evacuated.

Ramakheemya said that when their village was submerged in 1964, they moved to Mottegattu, a site close to their village. They lived there for two years. Later, the MLA brought them to this centre and asked them to settle here. Gurravaya from Kothapul-lareddipuram said, 'the Collector was camped in our village. He had made many promises, for instance, that the total amount of land lost will be compensated in the form of land itself. We were shifted during the first phase in 1959 as our village was close to the dam site. We were shown only this village and asked to settle here.'

Sarravaya from Gandhi Nagar, said, 'the Collector had told us that we would get 5 acres of land free of cost as well as house plots. He told us to select an area where we wanted to resettle.' These villagers visited Pullichintavagu, Timarpur, Serapalli and Gandhi Nagar. They selected Gandhi Nagar in 1966 because they were able to purchase 300 tadi trees for Rs 3,000 from a local person. Their main profession was the sale of *tadi*[3].

Villagers from Rajagattu said, 'three months before our village was submerged in 1964, the Special Collector tolds us that we have to vacate soon and can go wherever we want.' They visited four places but failed to find enough land anywhere. Finally, the Collector took two elders of the village to show them land at the main site, Rajagutta, and asked them to settle there. Peddabhuchram said, 'as there was not enough time, and also because everyone else was looking for land for rehabilitation and land was scarce, we decided to settle here.' But they refused to vacate their village till the date of submergence, holding on as long as they could. In fact, the authorities had to call in the army to force the villagers to vacate. Oustees now living in Shanti Nagar were aware of the displacement but refused to accept that it might happen. As their village was close to the dam site they were asked to vacate in 1959. The Collector and officials asked them to find a place for themselves but when they failed to comply they were shifted to Pedagutta which was close to their village. It took them two years to visit four or five resettlement sites themselves. Lakshmaya said, 'we decided to settle in Shanti Nagar because people told us that canal irrigation would soon reach this area. But we find that is not true as the canal only reaches Kalepalli.'

The Collector, *patwari* and *tehsildar* had held frequent meetings to appraise the oustees now living in Prem Nagar about their

---

[3] *Tadi*: Local intoxicating drink made from the juice extracted from palm trees.

displacement and relocation. In 1965, only three months before submergence, they asked the oustees to visit a few rehabilitation centres which the government had constructed. Venkaya told us, 'some of us wanted to settle in Pedagutta because it was close to our submerged village. But the others visited Narsapur and Prem Nagar and decided on the latter because it is close to Mirialguda town. Finally, all of us settled in Prem Nagar.' Of the 85 families who settled in Prem Nagar, only 15 now remain as the rest have left the area. The landed have sold their land to the local people and the landless have migrated to the command area.

Oustees living in Kothanandikonda centre told us that the *tehsildar*, *patwari* and Collector held more than 10 meetings to explain to them the details about their displacement and relocation. Anjhelu said, 'the Collector had promised that we would get free land, that arrangements for purchasing land would be made and house plots would be given to all the oustees. We were to be provided with irrigation facilities and a pond was to be constructed for cattle.' Bikshan said, 'the Collector had asked us to see the rehabilitation sites at Ulsyapalam, Narsapur, Jalapadu and Kothanandikonda in 1959. We visited the sites ourselves and chose this village because the Collector had promised that irrigation facilities would be provided. We shifted here in December 1960.'

Villagers from Kambalapalli had not been ready to vacate their submerged village because they felt that the compensation money given to them was not adequate. Although they visited Bhadrachalan, Wattanarkapalli and Mulkacherla, they did not select any land and continued to live in the village till 1963, when it was submerged. They were then forcibly evacuated by the army. The oustees, however, continued to live close to their village till 1964. Later, they chose Kambalapalli because by then there was not enough land available at any other centre.

Gasiya from Usmankunta Tanda centre said, 'our MLA, Shri G. Narain Reddy, had come with the Collector, *tehsildar* and *patwari* in 1965 and promised that we would get land free. Irrigation facilities would be provided and plots for houses given. But we had thought that we would not have to move. Three to four months before we shifted in 1966, we were asked by the Collector to settle in Usmankunta. We agreed.' Thanarya added, 'we did not resist because we were scared that we would be submerged. So we did what the Collector asked us to do without question.'

The Collector, *tehsildar* and the local MLA had told the oustees now living in Teldevalapalli that their village was to be submerged. Kanka Reddy said, 'even though we know about the submergence, we did not think that our village would be covered by water.' We had visited some villages in Mahboobnagar in Guntur district which had been earmarked for rehabilitation. Like the oustees now settled in Shanti Nagar, they too shifted from their submerged village to Pedagutta where they lived for two years because they had not decided where to resettle. As the Collector had specifically told them they could only settle in Nalgonda district, they opted for Teldevalapalli in 1966 as it was the closest site to their submerged village.

Compensation and Rehabilitation

Cash compensation was provided for the land and property acquired. Everyone was entitled to a house plot at the rehabilitation site. The landed were entitled to land which they either got free or had to buy depending upon the quantum of land lost. Besides, they were entitled to certain civic amenities. Although the state amendment to the Land Acquisition Act fixed the cash compensation to be awarded, there was no policy formulated for the rehabilitation of the displaced.

The Government of Andhra Pradesh had made a state amendment to Section 11 of the Land Acquisition Act, 1894, under the NSP Acquisition of Land Act (1956) dated 8 November 1956, to evaluate and acquire the agricultural land for monetary compensation.

To rehabilitate the oustees, the Irrigation Department of the Government of Andhra Pradesh issued a government order dated 3 July 1959 and a memo dated 16 August 1965. The Public Works Department of the Government of Andhra Pradesh issued a memo dated 19 January 1960. Thus, the entire process was governed by two memos and a government order.

According to the state amendment (8 November 1956):

a The market value of the land was fixed as on 1 July 1953.
b The value of any improvements to the land effected after the date and before the date of the publication of notification

under sub-section (1) of Section 4 of the Land Acquisition Act would be enquired into.

c The value of the land at the date of the publication of notification under sub-section (1) of Section 4 of the Land Acquisition Act would be enquired into.

Thus, the compensation would be evaluated at the market value as on 1 July 1953. This would also include any improvements made on the land or the value of the land as on the date of publication of Section 4 of the Land Acquisition Act.

The third point c stands in contradiction to the first and second points (a and b) because if the compensation evaluated was to include the value of land as on publication of sub-section (1) of Section 4 of the Land Acquistion Act, then a and b had no meaning. According to the government order, the oustees had to purchase land for resettlement at the market value as on 1 July 1953. It can then be said that compensation was paid at the market value on 1 July 1953. The state amendment was made after the foundation stone was laid in 1955 and the process of acquisition and displacement came even later. Yet, the fact that the compensation was to be calculated at the market value as on 1 July 1953 is in itself questionable.

According to information received from the oustees, they received, on average, compensation at the rate of Rs 100 to 150 per acre. They were given no explanation of the basis for this evaluation. The oustees living in Kambalapalli told us that although they had repeatedly protested against the compensation amount paid to them, the Collector had told them that they should accept whatever was given to them as he just did not have any more money to give.

Unaware as they were of the basis on which their land was evaluated, they were also unaware of whether they had been compensated for other assets such as trees and wells. Some of the oustees told us that they were not compensated for trees and wells. Although this could be true, no official records were available to cross-check this information.

All the oustees holding below 100 acres of land were given Rs 100 as a grant to meet the expenditure on reclamation of land as mentioned in the memo issued on 16 August 1965.

The oustees received Rs 300 to Rs 1,000 for *kuccha* and *pucca* houses, respectively. In addition to the compensation for the house (as per the memo dated 10 January 1960), the oustees who received less than Rs 750 were to receive the difference, with a ceiling fixed at Rs 300, as an ex-gratia payment.

However, our team was unable to corroborate this information as the officials at the dam site could not tell us where the official documents had been removed to.

LAND COMPENSATION

According to the government order dated 3 July 1959, and the memo of 16 August 1965, the landed oustees were either given land free of cost or were entitled to purchase it. This was determined according to the size of the landholding.

According to the Status Report (Government of Andhra Pradesh 1989), only 268 displaced families were landholders and 4,562 families were landless. A total of 29,506 acres of agricultural land was submerged. Therefore, each family's landholding would be approximately 100 acres. But our findings from 10 out of 23 rehabilitation centres indicated that prior to submergence 1,500 families had, on average, 10 to 15 acres of land and a few families had more than 20 acres. Nearly all of them have either received or purchased land as per the government order and the memo.

The government order of 3 July 1959 stated that those holding up to 20 acres were eligible to only 5 acres of dry land free of cost. Those oustees who had above 20 acres were entitled to purchase 5 acres of dry land at the market value as on 1 July 1953 (see Table 3.4).

In 1965, the government issued another memo which allowed people to buy land. This was to be in accordance with the land-holding lost and was over and above the entitlements covered by the government order of July 1959.

Thus, oustees holding between 5 to 10 acres were allowed to purchase 2.5 acres of dry land; those holding between 10 to 20 acres could purchase 5 acres of dry land, and those whose holdings exceeded 20 acres were entitled to purchase 7.5 acres more at the market value as on 1 July 1953 (See Table 3.4).

Although the people were entitled to purchase land, they were unable to do so. This was because the majority of the ousted

TABLE 3.4

Landholding	Entitled to land free of cost Acres	Entitled to buy land at market value (1 July 1953) Acres	Total Acres
Holding 5 acres or less	5.00	—	5.00
Holding between 5 to 10 acres	5.00	2.50	7.50
Holding between 10 to 20 acres	5.00	5.00	10.00
Holding above 20 acres	—	12.50	12.50

population had already shifted by 1965 and there was not enough land for them to purchase at the centres where they had resettled. The encroachers and the landless were not entitled to any land, only to house plots.

Even though the government order of July 1959 clearly stated that the oustees were entitled only to 'dry land' as compensation, this was not always the case.

At Rajagutta centre, six families received 4 acres of dry land and half an acre of 'wet' land. We were told that as they were being given some 'wet' land, they were entitled to a total of 4.5 acres of land instead of the stipulated 5 acres. Out of 100 families rehabilitated in Prem Nagar, 15 families received 5 acres of wet land as they were the first to settle in the area. By the time the remaining 85 families settled into the area, there was not sufficient wet land available. Therefore, these families got 4 acres of dry land and half an acre of wet land. However, oustees at the other eight centres were not as lucky. They received, or purchased, only dry land.

The gap of six years between the government order of 1959 and the memo of 1965 for grant of land has its own implications. The displacement of people had begun in 1959 and was almost complete by 1966. Of the 320 families who were entitled to purchase land, in the 10 centres we visited, only 75 families were able to do so. Fifty-four families who had also opted to purchase land did not succeed. This was due to the fact that the government issued the memo much after the people were rehabilitated and there was not sufficient land in the vicinity for them to purchase. Furthermore, to add to their misfortune, they lost the money they had deposited with the bank for the purchase of the land. Oustees had to first deposit the money in the bank and then present the receipt to the Collector who would then allot the land.

Gurravaya, son of Antaya from Kothanandikonda, had lost 31 acres of land due to submergence. He was entitled to buy 12.5 acres. He had deposited Rs 200 for 2.5 acres, over and above the 5 acres which he had already bought. But he did not get this land and in the process lost his money. The experience of C.M. Rammaiya, son of Mutaya from Kambalapally, is no different. He lost a total of 40 acres and he too was entitled to purchase 12.5 acres for which he deposited Rs 1,000. Instead, he received only 5 acres of dry land.

The other oustees at Kambalapally told us that they were unable to buy any extra land because there was just not enough land. Only, they had been judicious and not deposited any money for extra allotments. Rammulamma, a blind woman, told us that she had lost 26 acres of dry land. In return she was allowed to purchase only 5 acres of dry land which was not enough for her family. When she approached the officials for an additional 7.5 acres, she was told that there was no more land available for her to purchase. This drastic cut in the size of her holding forced her to encroach upon government land.

From Kothapullareddipuram, B. Mania Nayak told us that his father had 25 acres of land in the submergence zone. He could purchase only 5 acres at the rehabilitation centre as there was not enough land available. His father gave the 5 acres of dry land to Mania Nayak's younger brother, and Nayak too, with a family of children has been forced to encroach upon government land.

Not only was the allotted land inadequate, it was sometimes at a great distance from the centres. This made it difficult for the oustees to protect the fields and some lost their lands, as in the case of Muddavat Chenna who was forced to join the category of the landless. Others are still struggling to keep their lands from being usurped by the host population. The oustees resettled in Gandhi Nagar told us that their agricultural plot is 5 km away from their house plots but only half a kilometre from Apallegudum, Sityatanda, Lotiya Tanda and Gaddagud Tanda, villages occupied by non-oustees. The host villagers from these villages believe that they have been deprived of their grazing land by the new settlers and often let their cattle into the oustees' fields, thus destroying the standing crops.

CIVIC AMENITIES

According to the memo issued in 1960, the oustees were entitled to a plot of 10 cents for houses, free of cost. If they wanted bigger plots they could purchase an additional 15 cents. But once again, none of the oustees could purchase the extra land as there was no land available. The oustees were allowed to use the building materials from their previous houses for which they were provided transport facilities.

The memo also provided wells for drinking water, access to roads, centres and primary schools at each centre. The centres we visited had adequate drinking water facilities. At the time of displacement, three to four wells were constructed at each centre. To meet the increasing demand for water over a period of time, hand-pumps have since been installed.

Although unmetalled roads were constructed, transport facilities were not provided. Some centres like Gandhi Nagar, Rajagutta, Shanti Nagar and Kothanandikonda still do not have any transport facilities. The villagers have to walk 6 to 7 km to the nearest township. Kambalapally, Usmankunta Tanda and Teldevalapalli are not accessible during the monsoons for a period of four to five months when the unmetalled, *kuccha* roads fill up with water, making it impossible for buses to ply.

At all the 10 centres, schools up to the primary level were set up. However, here as in other rural areas, the system is much the same. As one oustee from Gandhi Nagar said 'the teachers have refused to come to teach in our village school because the village is in the interior and is not connected with the existing transport facilities.' Now the enterprising oustees have started to run private schools for their children and collectively pay the teachers their salaries.

The oustees living in Kambalapally, Usmankunta Tanda and Teldevalapalli have been denied all loan facilities. This, the officials have told them, is because they find it difficult to reach these interior villages to recover the loans.

There is, fortunately, no shortage of fuel and fodder as the villages are very close to the forest on which the people depend.

Impact of Displacement

The NSP proposed to change dry land into wet agricultural fields. This was, however, at the cost of the lives of 28,000 people who had to be uprooted for economic progress. But their 'displacement and rehabilitation' was given no thought.

The illiterate oustees were unable to foresee that their villages would be submerged. The oustees were mentally unprepared for displacement and made little effort to identify alternate lands. When they did begin to look for land they were left with very little time; some were forced to vacate their houses, others moved to higher slopes close to their old village, knowing well that they would eventually have to shift to an area alloted by the government. This left them feeling both unsettled and insecure.

The guidelines for 'compensation' and 'rehabilitation' did not provide oustees with a fair and just package. Land compensation calculated at the market value as on 1 July 1953 itself seems arbitrary because even the foundation-stone of the dam was laid two years later in 1955 and the process of acquisition began even later in 1957. A state amendment of Section 11 of the Land Aquisition Act (1894) was enforced to calculate the compensation for land. These criteria were not explained to the oustees. When some of them objected to the compensation amount, they were ordered to accept it without question. Many were left feeling that they were given much less than they were entitled to.

Although their lands were acquired to bring irrigation facilities to the region, the oustees were given only dry land. They had no share in the benefits. They were not even rehabilitated in the command area.

Certainly all those who were displaced were deeply affected. But it was the small and the marginal farmers and the landless who were the worst hit. The land compensation was inadequate. The majority of the oustees received only 5 acres of dry land. Some landholders like Muddavat Chenna have now been rendered landless and are dependent on wage labour.

The encroachers and the landless were not entitled to any land. Before displacement they were able to sustain themselves through sharecropping and by working as agricultural labourers within the village. But after displacement, they were left with no option but to look for alternative employment outside the village and the new site land was no longer sufficient to meet even the needs of the landholding families. Displacement and *ad hoc* rehabilitation measures made it inevitable for the majority of the oustees to migrate in search of daily wages.

Conclusion

The Nagarjunasagar project was initiated in 1955 and three and a half decades later, work on the distributary system is yet to be completed. The project was designed to irrigate 11.05 lakh hectares. Irrigation facilities from the project were made available for the first time in 1967. In 1986, however, the target was still elusive as the irrigated area was only 7.87 lakh hectares. Can one then consider the project as complete as the government claims?

The original estimate approved by the Planning Commission in 1960 was Rs 91.12 crores. By the end of the Seventh Plan, the cost had increased by a staggering 700 per cent to Rs 683.75 crores. To meet this increase the Andhra Pradesh Government had to take a loan of Rs 130 crores from the World Bank. Surely this negates any cost-benefit analysis that might have been made in 1955?

Approval of the original cost estimate by the Planning Commission came 5 years after construction work began. As always, the argument was that once the project is well underway, it will have to be completed because of the investment already made.

The project also had its impact on the health of the people. Studies reveal that large reservoirs are conducive to the spread of various water-borne diseases. Professor V. Ramalingaswamy, the then chief of the Indian Council of Medical Research has noted that a crippling bone disease, known as knock-knees, began to appear in Nagarjunasagar following the construction of the dam (Dogra 1984: 265).

The project displaced 5,098 families, fewer than other projects of similar magnitude. Yet, rehabilitation of even these few oustees received scant attention. Although construction work was initiated in 1955 and displacement began in 1958, the project authorities were not aware of the total number of families to be affected till as late as 1960. When the officials realised that a particular village was soon to be submerged, they asked the oustees to look for alternate land, thus giving them hardly any time to relocate themselves. The government had arbitrarily fixed 1 July 1953 as the cut-off date to calculate the amount of compensation to be paid. But the project was initiated two years later when the foundation stone was laid in 1955.

Government orders and memos clearly specified that oustees would receive or purchase 5 acres of dry land. In addition, they could purchase up to 12.5 acres, depending on the land lost due to submergence. These rules not only reduced the landholdings considerably, as there was not enough land at the rehabilitation site, but some like Muddavat were unable to protect their 5 acres from encroachment by the local population. With no share in the benefits, such oustees were completely marginalised and compelled to join the migrant labour force.

The NSP also submerged part of our history. Yet, painstaking efforts were made to excavate and preserve some of the Buddhist and Brahmanical monuments on the Nagarjunakonda Island. On the other hand *ad hoc* plans in the form of various orders, memos and state-amendments were all that governed the rehabilitation of the oustees, and in many cases even these rules were not implemented. Why is it that people like Muddavat Chenna are sacrificed in the name of progress? Is it not because their protest goes unheard? Would we in the cities suffer their fate if gold was discovered under a railway station?

References

Government of AP (Project Wing). 1989. *Report on NSP Left Canal and Dam.* March.

Subramanyam, S.K., Hanumanta Rao and **S.V. Rama Raju.** 1989. *Report on Socio-Economic Study of NSP.* Hyderabad: Centre for Economic and Social Studies.

Nagabhushanam, K. and **S.B. Surveshwar Rao.** 1969. *Report on Socio-Economic Study of Command Area.* Andhra University.

G.Lakshmi. n.d. Rehabilitation Policy for Andhra Pradesh Government: Nagarjunasagar to Srisailam (unpublished).

Dogra, Bharat. 1984. The Indian Experience with Large Dams. E.Goldsmith and N.Hildyard, ed., *The Social and Environmental Effects of Large Dams.* U.K.: Wadebridge Ecological Centre.

4

Resettlement and Rehabilitation of Dam Oustees: A Case-study of Ukai Dam

KASHYAP MANKODI

Introduction

There are several reasons why the case of the Ukai dam is especially interesting for a study of the involuntary resettlement of dam oustees. It is the largest man-made reservoir in the state of Gujarat where it is located. Although the nearby Sardar Sarovar project on the Narmada, which has been much more in the news, is far more ambitious both technologically and financially, it involves the partial or complete submergence of only 19 villages within the state of Gujarat. The Ukai dam submerged no less than 170 villages under the Vallabh Sagar reservoir created by it, a body of water covering an area of over 200 sq miles. The bulk of the areas submerged by the Sardar Sarovar are in states other than Gujarat.

However, since it is the Government of Gujarat which is responsible for the resettlement and rehabilitation of all oustees from

Note: This study is based on research carried out by the author in the project area since 1983 for the Centre for Social Studies, Surat and on his own subsequently.

the Sardar Sarovar project, the case of Ukai provides an insight into the track record of the government in the resettlement and rehabilitation (R & R) of displaced persons. Since there are significant differences in the context in which R & R in the two projects has been undertaken, it is to be hoped that the past performance of the government will not necessarily constrain its performance in future. However, the case of Ukai is a good example of how the planning and implementation of R & R projects in particular, and ambitious development projects which entail R & R in general, should *not* be done. It can therefore serve to warn developmental planners of reefs on which they can run aground.

The resettlement and rehabilitation of the population displaced by the construction of the Ukai dam, such as it was, reveals an almost complete lack of preparedness on the part of the government to approach a task of such magnitude. The response of the government to the problems arising from the forced relocation of thousands of families was totally inadequate. There was no well-planned policy to govern R & R, but only a series of executive fiats issued to address problems as they cropped up. Not only was the implementation of these callous and half-hearted but the policy-makers, planners and bureaucrats actually entrusted with the R & R of the oustees were neither aware nor concerned about the human and environmental consequences of involuntary resettlement on such a large scale.

As a result, the Ukai dam project had an extremely adverse environmental impact, to which the thoughtless felling of large tracts of forest for the resettlement of oustees contributed in no small measure. The economic, social and political costs (in terms of the redistribution of power) of both the multipurpose and irrigation projects as well as the R & R component were far higher than figures of the financial outlay would suggest. The lessons derived from this project therefore go beyond how or how not to resettle and rehabilitate populations displaced by surface irrigation or other developmental projects, but also pertain to the planning of multipurpose irrigation projects. These will be dealt with only in so far as they impinge on the primary objective of this study, which is to describe and analyse the displacement of the population by the construction of the Ukai dam, and the steps taken to resettle and rehabilitate those affected.

The following sections describe the background of the project and then the project itself. This is followed by an examination of the features of the area affected by the project, the R & R component and its fallout.

The Ukai Project

After Independence, there was a very strong demand from the states for clearance of river valley projects for which permission had to be obtained from the Planning Commission at the centre since the early 1950s. Under the circumstances, it was only natural that political pressure was brought to bear upon the centre to obtain this clearance. It may well have been so in the case of the Ukai project as well. The aim of irrigation planning in the early phase of planned development was to extend irrigation to those areas where it was not available and hence where agricultural production was limited. The paramount consideration was to grow more food.

The command area of the project, however, had an assured rainfall with an annual average ranging between 1,219 mm and 2,000 mm for different districts, and easy availability of ground water sources which already irrigated over 20,000 hectares within the command area. Consequently, irrigation from the project has been grossly underutilised, and has been used increasingly for cash crops at the expense of food crops, the production of which has steadily declined since the introduction of irrigation. Hence, there is good reason to believe that the project was sanctioned despite its incompatibility with the stated goals of irrigation development at the time. It is possible that the project was sanctioned as a *quid pro quo* for the support received from the affluent sections of the peasantry in the area during the nationalist movement. Sardar Patel, who was the first Home Minister and Deputy Prime Minister in the central government after independence, and after whom the reservoir created by the project was later named, was the hero of the peasants' struggle against British rule during the nationalist movement in the area which benefited from the project. It was the affluent section among these peasants who gained the most from the rapid development of water-intensive, high-return cash crops in the area at the cost of food crops.

Ukai was one project where the initial surveys—primarily for flood protection—had been carried out much earlier, in this case as far back as the end of the 19th century. However, a multipurpose river valley project including irrigation, hydroelectricity and flood protection had been visualised during the reconstruction plans after World War II, and initial surveys and investigations were then carried out. With the urgent necessity to extend irrigation immediately after independence and partition, this project was taken up soon after independence.

In the first phase, the project envisaged a weir at Kakrapar, 621 metres long and 14 metres high, which was completed in 1953. A 4,928 metre long and 68.6 metre high dam across the Tapti river near Ukai village, upstream from the Kakrapar weir, was envisaged in the second phase and completed in 1972. In subsequent stages a thermal power station near Ukai was completed, and a nuclear power station near Kakrapar is currently under construction. Though the displacement caused by the nuclear power station has had serious repercussions and led to a very tense situation in the recent past, we shall restrict our attention to the dam near Ukai which led to the formation of the 60 mile long and 3 to 4 mile wide Vallabh Sagar reservoir and the displacement of the population of 172 villages. Though the project visualised the creation of a 300 MW hydel potential and the protection of the lower Tapti basin, especially the city of Surat, from the devastating floods which had occurred frequently in the past, its most important component was the creation of a total irrigation potential of 3,86,000 hectares. Out of a total estimated cost of 1,146 million rupees for the second phase, 932.3 million rupees were earmarked for the irrigation component.

The project was taken up at a fairly low level of economic development, and in the context of chronic food shortages had two basic considerations: of increasing food production and reducing disparities in income. In the event, the project has actually decreased food production and sharply accentuated economic disparities, apart from having had a seriously adverse environmental impact. The utilisation of the irrigation potential created by it has been abysmally low. Although the generation of hydroelectricity has been higher than anticipated, this is due to the very low rate of water utilisation in the area upstream of the dam, caused in its turn by the serious economic dislocation of the area affected by submergence. The flood protection benefits offered by the dam may turn out in the long run to be much lower than claimed, and obtained at the cost of further disruption in the upstream area. Moreover, due to the extraordinarily high siltation rates in the reservoir as compared to the rates projected, the economic benefits accruing from its construction may be available for a much shorter period than anticipated, and thus prove to be far costlier than projected.

Before the resettlement and rehabilitation component of the project can be described in detail, it should be noted that the location of the dam already marked a boundary between two quite dissimilar areas, both in physiographical and economic terms. Upstream of Ukai, along the river which flows from east to west, the terrain is hilly, somewhat rocky, and was covered by forests till just before the project was completed, after which the forest cover disappeared almost completely within a very short period, thus exposing and eroding the precariously shallow top-soil. The population inhabiting this area subsisted primarily on agriculture and had depended quite heavily on forest produce, when it was available, to meet many of their basic needs. The developmental infrastructure available—roads, communications, electricity, social service—was already quite scanty and consequently, the people depended almost entirely on the land for survival. However, due to a favourable land-man ratio prior to submergence, the quality of life was reasonably good.

On the other hand, the area downstream of Ukai towards the west is flat, had deep and rich alluvial soil, was more densely populated and exceedingly well-serviced by transport and communication networks, other infrastructural components and services, and diversified economic opportunities arising from a much higher level of urbanisation and industrialisation. It was this area which had benefited most from the availability of irrigation, electricity, flood protection and other downstream benefits, not to mention the availability of cheap and plentiful labour, forced into seasonal distress migration from the upstream areas after the construction of the dam. The result of this disparity in levels of development has been not unlike the situation of the two brothers, in the popular children's story, who jointly inherited a cow, which the more powerful of the two apportioned such that he got the rear half which yielded milk and dung, while the weaker brother got the front half and had to constantly feed the cow and receive the attention of the cow's sharp horns. Since the Ukai cow firmly faces the east, it is suggested that apropos the downstream areas being called the *command* area, the upstream area should be called the *obey* area. In the following sections we shall examine the impact of the project exclusively on the obey area.

The Command and Obey Areas

Before considering the R & R component of the project in detail, it may be of interest to examine the differences between the command and obey areas in terms of the flow of benefits directly accruing from the project.

FLOOD CONTROL

It has already been noted that flood control benefits to the command area are available only at the cost of impounding more water and submerging larger portions of the obey area since the buffer capacity of the reservoir to absorb floods is limited by the need to keep it at a level adequate to meet the requirements of irrigation and hydroelectricity.

ELECTRICITY

The entire quantum of electricity generated is fed into the grid and diverted to areas other than the obey area, where there is a concentration of domestic and industrial consumers. In the obey area, electrical connections were available on a priority basis only for energising agricultural pumpsets, and not for domestic consumption. Potential consumers were required to dig a well and install a pumpset before a power connection or a subsidy for electric motors could be considered. Since the maximum land available to any agriculturist in the resettlement villages was less than 2 hectares, it was uniformly uneconomical to make the heavy investment required to irrigate such miniscule landholdings. Hence, those who made all the sacrifices so that more electricity could be generated were as a rule deprived of it. During the last few years a few connections have been made available in the resettlement

villages, but the negligible purchasing power of the resettled oustees continues to deny electricity to the bulk of the population.

IRRIGATION

Disparities in the availability of irrigation are even more pro-
nounced. The construction of the Ukai dam entailed the submergence of about 200 square miles under a reservoir which is
approximately 60 miles long and 3 to 4 miles broad. One hundred
villages were completely submerged and about 70 more were
partially submerged. As a result, 16,080 families, or a total population of about 52,000, were affected. Before the construction of the
dam these people cultivated the rich alluvial land on the river
banks where two crops could easily be grown without either extra
irrigation or fertilisers.

When these villages were rehabilitated, each landholder was
given a maximum of 4 acres of land in areas which were cleared of
forests for the purpose. Earlier, many persons had been cultivating
land that was not in their name, or, in several cases, large joint
family holdings were in the name of the head of the household
only. In these cases, only one title holder got a small plot of land.
The cultivators were promised help in building wells, improvement,
bunding, removal of free stumps and electricity. However, none of
these promises were actually fulfilled, resulting in a sense of betrayal.

Wells were not dug because of the official policy of providing
help to dig a new well only against every well submerged in the
reservoir. Since all the submerged villages had direct access to the
river earlier, wells had not been necessary in the old location of the
villages. Hence, no new wells were dug for the rehabilitated cultivators. Perhaps the most glaring example of a betrayal of the
oustees was the failure to successfully execute the promised lift
irrigation schemes. The callous attitude of the government
towards those people who had to sacrifice their lands in order to
increase the irrigation potential of the river is poignantly brought
out by the history of the lift irrigation scheme in Narayanpur, one
of the rehabilitated villages.

Narayanpur is situated close to the river Nesu where the back-
waters of the reservoir are available for lift irrigation. In 1968, a
600 metre RCC pipeline (2.5 metre long pipes of 0.5 metre dia-
meter) was laid and a tank was dug on top of a hillock from which

an estimated 800 acres could be irrigated by gravity flow. Nothing further was done for another 10 years. In 1978, when a pumphouse was built on the river bank and four electric motors with a combined capacity of 210 HP were installed, it was found that water could not be pumped up. The reason was that each of the 240 joints in the pipeline was so poorly sealed that there was massive leakage and water pressure could not be sustained to pump it up to the hilltop bank. More than 14 years after the inception of the lift irrigation scheme and after considerable expenditure had been incurred, it was still totally useless. This was true of each lift irrigation scheme taken up in the rehabilitated villages.

The hardship caused by the forced exchange of plentiful fertile land for small plots of land of poor quality and lack of irrigation was further compounded by mismanagement. The villagers claimed that although they could grow only one crop in their resettled villages for want of irrigation, the yield was adequate during the first few years. However, after four or five years the government levelled the newly cleared agricultural land with the help of bulldozers. The result of this operation was that all the accumulated humus and rich top-soil went into filling crevices and depressions and only rocky unproductive soil remained on top. Since no irrigation is available in the obey area, the use of fertilisers is not possible either and the people are forced to eke out a living from unproductive deforested land.

The sacrifice of local interest for the sake of progress or national interest can perhaps be justified, however tragic the localised consequences, if the larger interest can be shown to have been served. The question that arises then is whether or not the irrigation potential of the Ukai-Kakrapar scheme has been adequately and fruitfully utilised. The pattern of utilisation of the irrigation potential from this scheme therefore deserves close scrutiny.

The command area originally envisaged for the Kakrapar project was 3,45,209 hectares which were considered culturable, 22,750 hectares were grass and *khar* lands which did not utilise irrigation, about 20,000 hectares were under dry farming or alternative irrigation and 31,333 hectares were lying waste or fallow. Thus, only about 1,50,000 hectares were available for irrigation.

In the case of Ukai, the actual irrigation figures were less than those targeted but not significantly so, for the first three years. Thereafter, the development rate has not only been slow but has shown a reverse trend (Government of Gujarat n.d.: 2). It has to be remembered that against the culturable command area (CCA) of 1,52,400 hectares envisaged in the project report, the reappraised CCA in terms of which utilisation figures were obtained was only 1,19,330 hectares. During 1980–81 only 20,432 hectares were actually irrigated by the Ukai irrigation project. Is such a costly project justified in view of the utilisation observed since its implementation?

GENERATION OF EMPLOYMENT

Finally, there remains one benefit of development projects which has to be considered: the generation of employment. It may be argued in favour of such projects that they generate employment and are therefore desirable. However, even here, there is a tremendous difference in the repercussions of the project on the obey and command areas.

Informants in the obey area complained that they were suffering from forced idleness. Since they could only grow one crop during the year, agricultural operations, which usually kept most of them busy all the year round in their former villages, could only keep them busy for a short period in the new villages. Apart from agriculture some employment was available from forest operations and construction of roads and works, but it was quite insufficient. Besides these, there were two new areas of activity—cooperative marketing of milk and fish—which provided some employment. But even here a fraction of their needs could not be met by these opportunities. Furthermore, the common factor in both these operations was the outflow of nutritive foodstuffs which had earlier been available for local consumption. In the export of fish from the area, middlemen and transport contractors also tended to corner large profits. Apart from these, there simply was nothing for the people to do. This forced unemployment generated its own social problems.

SOCIAL EVILS

One result of this has been an increase in the incidence of social evils like drunkenness and gambling. Our informants claimed that due to forced idleness a greater number of people tend to indulge in drinking. In one village (Tokarwa), we found that some outsiders who were settled in the rehabilitated villages had lost their license for a fair price shop following malpractices. Instead, they were operating a *matka* (number gambling) ring which systematically soaked up a fair part of the cash available from new economic activities like the marketing of milk or fish.

MIGRATION

Village leaders claimed that in their former villages the villagers could hardly meet their own labour requirements. It was suggested that this was responsible for the practice of polygamy. After displacement however, there had been a massive increase in the number of unemployed and demoralised. In Narayanpur, about 2,000 out of the total population of 6,000 stay away from the village for up to eight months in the year. In some of the other villages—Kataskuwa, Dhupi, Arkati, Kuida, Adgam, Kuchal, Panibara, Mohini, Chandipur—it was found that between one-third and over three-fourths of the huts were closed and sometimes sealed. These belonged to those who had been forced to migrate in search of work 'to Gujarat', as the villagers explained. In Dhupi, the primary school teacher said that out of 25 children in his school, only about 10 were present in the village. All the others had accompanied their parents who had migrated in search of work.

Overseers from these villages hire labourers who are given some rations, occasionally material for building huts and some cash in advance. The overseer gets 11 per cent from the employers in the command area as his labour contract commission, and whatever else he can derive from the conversion of cash wages into kind. Since the first phase of fieldwork during October coincided with the onset of the sugar-cane cutting season, we were able to observe the movement of very large numbers of people.

During our stay in the obey area villages, about one and a half to two dozen trucks loaded to capacity with labourers passed daily down the Nizar-Ucchal road. Large wayside camps of migrant labourers were also visible between Bardoli and Ucchal. There were caravans of close to 100 bullock carts, and trains packed both inside and above with migrant labourers from Khandesh. In Ucchal, a fleet of 28 private chartered buses was waiting to transport workers to the sugar-cane fields and factories in the command area. Tractor trailers were also frequently used to transport workers. We were told that at the onset of the monsoon these labourers return to the villages with what remains of the few hundred rupees that constitute their wages and bonus, after spending heavily on alcohol and the purchase of transistor radios. They eke out the four months of the monsoon season in their inhospitable rehabilitated villages.

Thus, as in the case of the benefits of irrigation, electricity and flood control, the generation of employment also favoured the command areas at the cost of the obey areas. A decade after the completion of the project there was nothing for the displaced to do, whereas the industrial or agricultural capitalists in the command areas were favoured with an unending and, perforce, unorganised supply of cheap migrant labour to exploit.

Rehabilitation Under the Ukai Project

The total land acquired under the project was spread over two districts in Gujarat—Surat and Bharuch—and one district—Dhulia—in Maharashtra. A total of 170 villages were affected due to the project. The acquired land was needed for the large reservoir basin, the dam seat and project colonies. For the purpose of estimating land under submergence a full reservoir level of 105.16 metres or 345 feet was taken into account. The area of land acquired thus totalled 60,802 hectares. The land between the full reservoir level and a high flood level of 106.98 metres was not acquired, but the dwellings located in this area were shifted elsewhere.

For the purpose of acquiring land and facilitating rehabilitation of the affected population, a special organisation headed by an Additional Collector and supported by revenue staff was created. According to a resolution of the government dated 29 November 1968, an Advisory Committee for Rehabilitation was also formed under the chairmanship of the Additional Collector. The Committee members included the rehabilitation officers, Ukai Executive Engineer, the Registrar of Cooperatives Societies, the Superintending Agricultural Officer, Presidents of District Panchayats, and prominent local leaders and representatives of voluntary social organisations. This Committee met from time to time to advise the government about rehabilitation.

Of the 170 villages affected by the reservoir, 100 were fully submerged while the remaining were partially submerged. According to official estimates, a total of 16,080 families were affected by the project. Of these, 14,148 families were rehabilitated in 17 groups of settlements, whereas the remaining 1,932 families moved away on their own after accepting *ad hoc* grants. Thus, 138 villages were rehabilitated in 17 groups of resettlements.

Land acquired for the project was only a part of the total land affected by the project. As already mentioned, 60,802 hectares were acquired. However, the total area affected even at full reservoir level (not high flood level) was as follows:

Occupied agricultural land   30,352 hectares
Government wasteland   11,568 hectares
Government forest land   22,258 hectares
Total   64,178 hectares

Over and above this, 7,378 hectares of forest land were cleared and actually distributed for agricultural purposes.

Provisions for Land Acquisition and Rehabilitation

The following is a brief summary of the various government resolutions under which land was acquired from the oustees and compensation paid, and the arrangements for the setting up of resettlement colonies made. The relevant government resolution numbers and dates are given in parentheses at the beginning of each paragraph.

DEPARTMENT OF AGRICULTURE AND COOPERATION: FLD 1666/70, P. 297 OF 4 OCTOBER 1967)

According to this resolution, the conditions under which cleared forest land was sold to agriculturists whose lands were acquired for the project were determined as follows:

Area of land acquired	*Area of land made available in new settlements*
Up to 3 acres	Actual area acquired
3 to 9 acres	3 acres
9 to 12 acres	One-third of actual area acquired
More than 12 acres	4 acres

This area of land made available for agricultural purposes after clear-felling forests was to be sold at an appropriate price determined by the government. For the purpose of paying compensation to those landholders whose lands were acquired, the acquired lands were classified into four categories according to the land revenue criteria for different *talukas*. These compensation paid included a 15 per cent solatium, and ranged between Rs 600 to 960 per acre for different categories of land. For wasteland the compensation paid was only Rs 40 per acre.

(JMN-3966-3334-A, 1 AUGUST 1967; MPW 9263-46 OF 14 JANUARY 1966; REH 4966-K-1 OF 7 OCTOBER 1967)

The exact extent of area submerged was not determined at the time and the waterspread of the reservoir would vary, depending upon the rainfall in the catchment areas and the water released from the dam for utilisation. These resolutions therefore determined the conditions under which cultivation of the reservoir banks could be practised.

Till such time as the acquired land was not submerged, former owners were allowed to cultivate it on an annual basis after paying double revenue and various other taxes. Agriculturists whose lands were under submergence were to be given preference for bed/bank cultivation. The maximum area for bed/bank cultivation thus made available was 3 acres. There was a limit on the total area of land to be cultivated. The agriculturists could cultivate a total of 16 acres of land, inclusive of all their other lands. Bed cultivation was to be allowed normally on an annual basis with the possibility of triennial leases where the lands remained unsubmerged for long periods. The land revenue collected from such plots was 12 times the normal rate and no compensation or revenue exemption could be claimed in the event of any damage to crops due to floods in such plots. If the acquired land remained unsubmerged for longer periods, it could be returned to the former owners on a refund of compensation paid to the government.

(MIP 4767/4–K OF 28 NOVEMBER 1967)

Landholders could avail of loans at 6 per cent interest through the Ukai Navnirman Sangh, a voluntary social organisation for the purchase of additional land up to a maximum of 8 additional acres.

(MIP 2267/2906–K OF 1 JULY 1963;
PWD MIP 2263/2906–K OF MARCH 1968;
PWD REH 4967 (6) 1 OF 7 OCTOBER 1967;
PWD NIO 4965/K OF 3 FEBRUARY 1968;
REH 4967/K (I) OF 7 OCTOBER 1967)

These resolutions laid down the conditions for the erection of alternative dwellings for the oustees. Oustees who were landowners were to be given residential plots 80 feet by 40 feet, and those who did not own land were to be given plots of 40 square feet. Transportation of belongings, including construction materials, was to be provided free of cost to the oustees by the government, provided the value of the construction material to be transported was less than Rs 5,000 and relocation was done within the stipulated period. Loans for building new houses were available at 7 per cent up to a maximum of Rs 4,000 and, in exceptional cases, Rs 5,000 provided they conformed to certain standards. Extra plots could be purchased by the oustees for use by family members under certain conditions.

A well was to be constructed in the new settlement for every hundred persons to be rehabilitated, with watering facilities for cattle.

(MIP 4964/77775–K OF 2 MARCH 1967)

Some land in every resettled village was to be reserved for public purposes like crematoriums, manure pits, playgrounds, the village panchayat and *balwadi* buildings.

(MIP 4964 (4) K OF 17 JANUARY 1966)

Approach roads and connecting roads with the necessary culverts and other appartenant works were to be provided to the resettled villages.

(TDB 1075.4.0 314 C: OF 7 OCTOBER 1965)

Schools and other public buildings existing in the affected villages prior to 1964 would be replaced in the resettlement villages. In those villages where such facilities could not be obtained, demands for such public buildings were to be considered on a priority basis by the relevant district panchayats.

(GHM 76 M/S T.C.P. 1066/30496 OF 5 JANUARY 1967)

This resolution granted oustees exemption from stamp duty that could be levied on agreements signed.

(NSC 1266–5880–K OF 21 OCTOBER 1967)

For those who were willing to undergo training in certain crafts training classes in carpentry, masonry, turning and fitting, tailoring, and blacksmithying were started in Ukai. A monthly scholarship of Rs 30 and free accommodation were also offered.

(REH 4968–4207 (3)-K OF 13 DECEMBER 1968)

Those oustees who would prefer to arrange for their own rehabilitation were offered the following cash grants:

For every landless family	Rs 450
Landholding families not eligible for land in resettlement villages	Rs 550
Landowning families eligible to get land in resettlement villages	Rs 670

These grants could be paid after the oustees relinquished possession of their earlier dwellings. Such families were not eligible to receive any other rehabilitation facilities.

These resolutions, which were passed by the government over a period of five years and five months, reveal the piecemeal character of the rehabilitation effort at Ukai. Even a cursory perusal of these resolutions shows that in the government's attitude the iron fist is far more evident than the velvet glove. Before commenting on some of the provisions of these resolutions pertaining to rehabilitation, let us examine what was offered to those oustees who, for some reason, did not wish to accept the government's help and generosity in rehabilitating them. Such families who were uprooted from their traditional habitats, who had to leave behind the security of their land, houses, social relationships and customary occupations and face the uncertainties of life in a strange land among strangers, were offered the princely sum of Rs 450 to Rs 670 as a reward for cooperating with the government. With this they had to fend for themselves as their acceptance of this reward made them ineligible for any other facilities offered by the government for rehabilitation.

The irony is that given the quality of rehabilitation offered, these voluntary refugees were not necessarily worse off in their homeland than those who were rehabilitated by the government. The provisions of rehabilitation can be discussed under three heads: land, dwellings and other facilities offered in the new settlements.

Land

The compensation offered was quite inadequate, considering the quality of land acquired. The acquired land was mostly fertile, enriched as it was by the silt deposited on the river banks. It was also well-drained and capable of yielding multiple crops even without irrigation or fertilisers, and landholdings tended to be large and viable. Against this, the land offered in return was far too inadequate to be economical. Moreover, it was land from which the forest cover had been removed almost overnight, and instead of being constantly enriched, it was vulnerable to the ravages of the elements and continuous impoverishment. It could not be a substitute for the land that was acquired.

Apart from cultivating the deforested land offered in return, the oustees could also cultivate the exposed bed of the reservoir when the water receded from the banks in the dry season. To begin with, the decision to expose the banks of the reservoir to erosion due to cultivation instead of securing the soil by covering it with some appropriate species of vegetation where possible, is questionable. However, this bed cultivation was not allowed in order to mitigate the blow of uprootment on the oustees. The government's calculation becomes clearer when we take into account the punitive revenue that was proposed to be levied for bed cultivation. The oustees' hunger for land was thus meant to be turned to profit.

Dwellings

The oustees were to be exempted from paying stamp duty on their agreements with the government. However, as in the case of free transportation offered to shift their belongings, this was due less to any generosity on the part of the government and more to suit its own convenience. Exemption from stamp duty and free transportation to the resettlement colonies would ensure smoother legal and physical relocation. This becomes clearer when we notice that free transportation had a condition attached to it: that it was to be available only if the oustees were to follow the government's schedule for shifting. Free transportation for construction materials was subject to a maximum value of Rs 5,000, as was the loan available for building new houses in the resettlement colonies. The new houses built were thus of very inferior quality. Moreover, no electricity was provided for domestic use or for illuminating public places.

Other Facilities

By and large, the facilities provided in the resettlement villages were inadequate. Only in one village (Kamlapur) did we find that the availability of drinking water had improved after resettlement. Some of the roads provided in the resettlement colonies—for instance, the road joining village Tokarwa with the reservoir bank from where a ferry service to the north bank is available—are completely unusable due to poor construction and maintenance.

We have already seen earlier how none of the lift irrigation schemes are working and how land levelling has done more harm than good.

Considering that most facilities in the resettlement villages are in a state of neglect and chronic disrepair, one wonders how serious the govenment was about offering a reasonable infrastructure to the resettlement colonies. For instance, in order to combat the large-scale unemployment that was bound to result from the shrinking of the land base on which the ousted communities survived, the government offered two schemes. One was to provide any rehabilitated person who asked for it with a certificate to the effect that he or she had been affected by the Ukai dam. The other was the training classes in some crafts started at Ukai, where the trainees were to be paid a stipend of a mere Rs 30 a month.

In sharp contrast to the dry, dusty and bleak rehabilitation colonies are the lush gardens and lawns and the well-lit and more than comfortable dwellings provided at the dam site, where those who plan, build, maintain, and benefit from the project live. This striking contrast between the rehabilitated and the rehabilitators is not project-specific. Our enquiries reveal that in the Sardar Sarovar project on the Narmada, the estimated cost of buildings alone (i.e., without any other infrastructural facilities) in Kevedia colony, which is only one of several, is Rs 23.6 crores, with a further estimated cost of Rs 25 crores for maintenance and furnishing. This will house the rehabilitators for a few years. As against this, the total cost for different components of the rehabilitation programme which will permanently uproot a population several times that of Kevedia colony is Rs 9 crores. Our argument is that this disparity between those who rehabilitate and those who are rehabilitated cannot continue indefinitely without endangering the social order.

A final word about the rehabilitation effort at Ukai is in order, before examining its cost in detail. This has to do with the role of voluntary agencies in rehabilitation. It was observed at Ukai that the *sarvodaya* organisation, the Ukai Navnirman Sangh, played a very important role in facilitating rehabilitation. This organisation helped the government at practically every stage and was given official recognition by the government. Its representatives were included on the Advisory Committee for Rehabilitation and grants for the purchase of extra land by the oustees were rented through it. The dedication of its workers and the rapport they established with the oustees is visible even now in the large number of schools started by the organisation in the resettlement colonies.

Since no thorough socio-economic-cultural survey of the oustees was done prior to rehabilitation, the result of this effort to help the government with rehabilitation was in some respects unfortunate. When the oustees were given cash sums through the mediation of the voluntary organisation, the real beneficiaries of the scheme turned out to be the traders and money-lenders of the nearby trading town of Navapur, and not the oustees who were the intended beneficiaries. This was because the oustees were unfamiliar with handling large amounts of money as their economic trans-actions had mostly been in the nature of barter or direct exchange of commodities and services.

It is conceivable that the role of well-meaning voluntary agencies in assisting the government with rehabilitation might change for the better. In future, voluntary agencies might hesitate to unques-tioningly help the government with facilitating rehabilitation, even if they accept the implementation of a given hydel-irrigation project as a *fait accompli*. Instead of acting as the oil which the govern-ment can spread over waters that may become troubled, they may conceivably bring home to those who are likely to be ousted in future the real nature of rehabilitation, and thus help in fomenting what would appear to governments as 'trouble'. Only after a more enlightened and human rehabilitation policy is evolved and sought to be implemented can such agencies be expected to work in tandem with governments again.

Aspects of the Cost of Resettlement and Rehabilitation

The official estimate of the total outlay for the rehabilitation for oustees of the Ukai project stood at Rs 123.1 million. Upward revisions of cost in successive project estimates are as chronic a feature of irrigation projects in India as delays in construction schedules and time overruns. Since the figure quoted was arrived at when the project was commissioned and since litigation regarding claims for enhanced compensation continued for a long time after, there is no reason to believe that the figure represents an immutable and authoritative index of the cost, the resettlement and rehabilitation componen's of the project. The likely changes in the figure due to the settlement of such claims are, however, quite insignificant compared to those which may be necessitated by scrutinising the basis on which such cost estimates are arrived aι.

Several questions arise in connection with the determination of the basis on which estimates of the cost of rehabilitation are arrived at. Accounting procedures for outlay or expenditure on rehabilitation need not necessarily accurately reflect either the size of the hole in the taxpayer's pocket or the cost to society as a whole. Besides obvious lacunae like the omission of the cost of administrative overheads or of the quantifiable economic setbacks received by the resettlers beyond the compensation of their acquired assets, there are less visible aspects like the estimation of the damage demonstrably caused to the physical environment as a direct result of poor rehabilitation, or the strain on the polity due to a manifestly unjust distribution of the pains and gains of development. Pauperisation due to badly planned and executed involuntary resettlement programmes may entail an unquantified but undeniable cost of environmental degradation and a similar one of socio-political deterioration which affect not only those who directly bear such costs but everyone, including those who might appear to be direct beneficiaries. This may upset all calculations regarding a seemingly acceptable trade-off between high costs and high returns.

The most common argument offered in favour of the costs of inadequate rehabilitation and the resulting pauperisation of resettlers is that even if some people suffer, an equal or larger number gain directly as a result. Thus, high costs *per se* mean nothing if they are localised and offset by a more generalised distribution of higher net gains. This argumen² can be countered by showing both that a more rational calculation of costs may offset seemingly higher net gains and by pointing out that the high costs may not be localised after all. A pauperised resettler who is forced to destroy forests or to turn to crime in order to survive is not only bearing the cost himself, but passing it on to others as well, in that a large number of people may be consumers of the benefits offered by forests, or by public order and freedom from crime. The not so clearly visible effects of growing disparities between the losers whose aspirations may be simultaneously enhanced, and the gainers who may be further alienated from the less privileged, may turn out to be far more serious in the long run than is evident at the outset.

In order to complete the argument that even if the overall social cost of the project is high enough to offset a much larger part of its benefits than may seem to be the case, i.e., even where the benefits actually achieved do closely approximate those promised or planned (which is demonstrably not the case), it is necessary to consider three things. The changes in the socio-economic condition of the oustees due to resettlement is the first of these. The second is the outlay that would be required to restore these conditions at least to their former level. And finally, the indirect ecological cost of the project, especially of its resettlement component is important. This exercise would also be presupposed for any rational calculation of the real cost of resettlement and rehabilitation for a given unit and the exploration of cost-effective alternatives.

Prior to their submergence, the villages affected by the project were located in the Tapti basin on fertile land drained by the rivers Nesu, Rangawali and Raigan, and some other tributaries of the Tapti, along with many smaller streams. The gentle undulations of the Satpura range through which the Tapti flows westwards were thickly forested prior to the construction of the dam by both moist and dry deciduous forests which covered 49 per cent of the area. With an annual average rainfall of about 55 inches, a fertile and drained soil, and a protective cover of well-preserved forests which regulated the percolation and discharge of sub-soil water, these villages had developed a rich and stable agricultural and horticultural base. The fields and orchards were famous for their quality produce which enjoyed pride of place in the court of far-off Delhi, even in Mughal times, according to historians. Multiple cropping and a sensible pattern of crop rotation involving cereals and legumes ensured large and stable yields and prevented soil exhaustion.

A scrutiny of land utilisation statistics in the different administrative divisions of this area reveals that with the construction of the dam the primary means of production in an agrarian economy, namely land, was nearly halved when about 44 per cent of the agricultural land was submerged, on average, for an affected area. In some administrative divisions only a tiny fraction—approximately 13 per cent—of the agricultural land was submerged. Agriculture being the mainstay of the economy, as much as 95 per cent of the workforce of the affected area was dependent on land, according to census statistics.

The economy of the affected area was not only marked by an exceptionally high dependence on land but also had a distinct pattern of landholding. Landholdings were, as a rule, much larger in the affected area than in Surat district as a whole. Secondly, the pattern of the ownership of land was far less skewed than elsewhere. Landholdings by size and class were distributed much more evenly in the affected area. For Surat district as a whole, 55 per cent of the landholdings were small, i.e., under 5 acres, whereas only 22 per cent of the landholdings in the affected area were small and there were as many, or more, medium and large landholdings. Thus, 23.60 per cent of landholdings in the affected area were larger than 15 acres.

After the submergence of more than half of this rich agricultural area, the largest landholding that any agriculturist could have was a mere 4 acres. Whereas earlier, agriculturists could grow enough food to meet all their requirements and generate a surplus which was large enough to comfortably support the entire population of landless, this was no longer possible after submergence and resettlement.

Earlier studies had revealed low levels of education, exposure to the outside world, motivation for occupational change, and particularistic contacts outside the area and, therefore a general unwillingness to migrate outside the area, even among the landless. Surveys carried out by this author 10 years after resettlement revealed a regular cycle of seasonal distress migration under which between half and more than three-fourths of the population of the resettled villages migrated for work outside the area. This had serious repercussions on the development of the economy and on education in the affected area, besides exposing the helpless migrant population to exploitation in the receiving areas.

Due to the shrinking land base, there was an increase in the unauthorised cultivation of forests and other public lands, which further degraded the already devastated environment of the area. But this did not prevent 95 per cent of the population in the affected area from having to subsist below the poverty line, drawn at the consumption level of Rs 60 per capita per month, according to a study carried out in 1980 (Jain 1980: AFP 5). The nutrition of the resettled population suffered badly as a result of the drastic reduction in intake of fruit, vegetables, and animal proteins, since the ravaged land could no longer support enough livestock or game. The availability of fish did increase due to pisciculture in the newly-built reservoir but fish became a marketed commodity instead of an item of consumption. Increase in fish yields was hardly reflected in the diet of the affected population. Conversely, there was an increase in alcoholism, gambling, and crimes against property. Due to the almost complete deforestation of the area, those communities which earlier subsisted on economic activities dependent on forest produce were the worst hit. Resettlement also led to a marked deterioration in the quality of housing and in relationships within the family as well as the community.

Besides, there were other subtle but equally regrettable and irreversible socio-economic changes which do not easily lend themselves to quantification. The availability of transport and communications, educational facilities and drinking water for some resettled villages did improve, but increased education and exposure without any other economic avenues for vertical mobility only served to raise levels of aspiration as well as frustration. Micro-level planning exercises carried out in the area have revealed two things. First, that the minimum necessary per capita expenditure for economic reconstruction would be approximately Rs 1,200 over a five year period. Second, that given the average household size observed over a large and representative sample, the displaced population must have been close to 95,000 and not 52,000 as officially claimed. It would then appear that the cost of remedial development to undo the damage done by resettlement and poor rehabilitation would be about Rs 110 million, which would need to be added to the official outlay of Rs 123 million on rehabilitation. The ecological cost of deforestation necessitated by rehabilitation alone may be worked out on the basis of official statistics and some conservative assumptions at well over Rs 300 million additionally.

Is this costly exercise, in the absence of an enlightened and standard rehabilitation policy and its imaginative and sincere implementation, capable of performing the basic function of a social policy: to protect the social order from possible disruption, to enable economic development to continue without any breakdown in the system?

References

Government of Gujarat. n.d. *Final Report of the Committee of the Panel on Integrated Land and Water Use on Underutilisation of Irrigation Potential in. Respect of Ukai and Kakrapar Project*. Gandhi Nagar: Irrigation Department.

Jain, S.C. 1980. *Block Level Planning: Ucchal Taluka*. Vol. I. South Gujarat University.

5

The Oustees of Pong Dam: Their Search for a Home

RENU BHANOT • MRIDULA SINGH

Introduction

The year was 1970. The construction work on the Pong dam was approaching its end. The overall atmosphere was one of eager expectancy. After all, the completion of the project by 1974 was to metamorphose the dry lands of Rajasthan into lush green fields and also benefit some parts of Punjab and Haryana. It was going to speed up the process of industrialisation as well.

However, this vision became clouded as without warning almost 4,000 people marched to the dam site. Having been forced to leave their houses, they were protesting because no alternate plans had been made for their resettlement.

Note: The fieldwork for this study was done by Kavaljit Singh, Sandeep Mahalanobis, Renu Bhanot and Mridula Singh. The first draft of this paper based on individual reports, was written by Renu Bhanot.

This study would not have been possible without the help and guidance of Mr S.D. Randhawa, Secretary PDOA which is actively involved in the post rehabilitation problems of the oustees. We are also grateful to all the oustees for their help and hospitality. We also owe our gratitude to Mr V.N. Singh, Mr Hari Shanker, Mr K.K. Pathania, Mr Prem Chand Attree, Mr D.C. Randhawa and Mr C.R. Prem.

The protest continued for 15 days, during which time work at the site came to a halt. After several rounds of negotiations with the Pong dam oustees' Samiti (PDOS)[1] the project authorities promised them proper rehabilitation in the command area of the dam in Rajasthan.

It was now 1985. The Pong Dam Oustees' Association (PDOA) had raised questions in the Lok Sabha regarding the condition of the oustees: a Had the government reserved the total area required for resettlement as per the agreement between the two state governments of Himachal Pradesh and Rajasthan under the supervision of the central government? b Were the allotments being made out of the reserved area? c Was it known to the government that the oustees were being harassed by unsocial elements? and d What were the steps being taken to improve the situation?

In response, the then Minister for Power stated that 2.25 lakh acres of command land had been reserved by 1970 and the allotments were being made out of this area alone. He added that the law and order problem was limited to a few cases of illegal encroachment and the state government was intervening promptly in the matter.

The same set of questions was once again raised in the Lok Sabha as recently as in 1990. The replies were no different either. Only this time, it was the Minister of Energy who fielded the questions.

That the main concern of the project authorities lies in the benefits from the project and that the affected persons figure is last on their list of priorities has by now been conclusively established. Small wonder then that a substantial number among them find their existence reduced to a relentless struggle for survival. Their plight worsens in an inter-state project. In such cases, responsibility for resettlement is shuttled between one state and the other while all the states concerned compete for the highest share of benefits.

The present study on the Pong dam forms an important link in a series of studies. This project was chosen primarily to study the manner in which rehabilitation of the oustees was achieved. The displacement of people began in 1966 and was said to have been

---

[1] The Pong Dam Oustees Samiti is not synonymous with the Pong Dam Oustees Association. The former was a hasty conglomeration of some local leaders and it broke up shortly afterwards.

completed by 1972–73. But in 1989, when this study was undertaken, the process of resettlement was nowhere near completion;
more than half the displaced families from Himachal Pradesh had
still to be resettled.

The case-study on the Pong dam, an inter-state project, has
other dimensions as well. The families displaced from Himachal
were resettled in Rajasthan, a state that was socially, culturally
and climatically very different from their own. One of the major
problems they confronted after resettlement was hostility on the
part of the host population.

The main demand of the displaced of every project is to be given
a share in the benefits generated from the project which displaces
them. The Pong dam, therefore, made an interesting study as the
oustees were rehabilitated in the command area of the project.
This, supposedly, was to help them regain their lost livelihood.

The Project

The idea of a dam across the river Beas was first mooted in 1926 by
the Punjab government. A Committee was formed in 1927 to
explore the possibilities of storing the surplus waters of the river.
A report recommending the type of dam to be built was submitted,
but the project authorities took no action and the matter rested
there.

Following the Indo-Pak Treaty of 1957 which conferred on India
the right to full utilisation of the waters of the three eastern rivers,
Ravi, Beas and Sutlej, interest in a dam across the Beas was
revived, leading to a second round of investigations.

Though the preliminary report based on these investigations
recognised the power potential of the project, it did not envisage
power generation as its prime objective. The project was planned
for irrigation purposes alone. The sharing of benefits between
Punjab, Rajasthan and Haryana was also not clearly laid down in
the report.

A more detailed and systematic feasibility study was finally
undertaken. This was based on the various alternatives suggested
in earlier reports and on the advice of the United States Bureau of
Reclamation. The final report, in 1959, suggested that a hydroelectric project could be constructed.

Large tracts of agricultural land, especially in Rajasthan, were mainly dependent on erratic rainfall. Therefore, the need to harness the large volume of monsoon water that was otherwise going waste was recognised. It was thought that a major dam over the Beas would help provide Rajasthan with perennial irrigation.

Exploitation of the power potential of the project was seen as the only way to industrial development in the absence of other sources of power in the region.

Floods were more or less a regular feature, especially in Punjab. Though not a prime objective, the idea of controlling the severity of floods served as an added incentive in the Pong dam multipurpose project.

Some Relevant Facts About Pong Dam

The dam across the river Beas is at the foothills of the Shivalik Range and is located at village Pong in Dehra Gopipur *tehsil* of Kangra district in Himachal Pradesh.

Name	Pong Multipurpose Dam
Maximum height	435 ft (132.59 metres)
Full reservoir level	1,421 ft (433.12 metres)
Normal reservoir level	1,400 ft (426.72 metres)
Length of reservoir	41.8 km (26 miles)
Dead storage level	1,260 ft (383.05 metres)
Gross storage capacity	6.95 maf (8,570 million cum)
Live storage capacity	5.91 maf (7,290 million cum)
Name of the canal	Rajasthan Canal (now called Indira Gandhi Canal)
Length of the canal	649 km
Length of distributaries	6,500 km

EXPECTED BENEFITS

a Power
   Total Installed Capacity   360 MW
b Irrigation Potential
   Total   4 million acres

c Distribution of Power and Irrigation

State	Power (in per cent)	Irrigation
Rajasthan	58.5	3 million acres
Punjab	24.9	—
Haryana	16.6	1 million acres
Total	100	4 million acres

BENEFITS GENERATED

No data was available regarding the benefits actually generated since the project began.

In 1966, the state of Punjab was reorganised and Himachal Pradesh was formed. As a result, the submergence zone of the dam (falling in district Kangra) became a part of the new state. The benefits of the dam were to be distributed between Rajasthan, Punjab and Haryana. The newly constituted state of Himachal Pradesh, the state which donated the land for the project was, however, not allocated any share in the benefits. Why not is a question that keeps recurring.

The construction of the dam commenced in 1961 and was completed by 1974. The FRL (Full Reservoir Level) of the dam was 433.12 metres. However, only the land to be permanently submerged up to a level of RL 429 metres was acquired. The project authorities had stated that the chances of damage to land above this level, i.e., between 429.75 metres and 433.12 metres, were extremely remote. They had, therefore, considered it more beneficial to leave that area for cultivation. In the eventuality of the water level exceeding 429.75 metres, to compensate the damage to the standing crops was thought to be a better option than to acquire all the land (Rehabilitation of Displaced Persons at Beas Dam Project, 1986).

The reservoir submerged 71,724 acres, inclusive of private land belonging to 30,000 families, i.e., a population of 1,50,000 spread over 94 villages comprising 316 *tikkas*[2] in Nurpur and Dehra

---

[2] According to the official source, a *tikka* is a revenue estate. Each village comprises more than one *tikka* or revenue estate.

Gopipur *tehsils* of Kangra district. Out of the 316 *tikkas*, 124 were fully submerged and 192 were partially affected.

Different government reports give contradictory data. For instance, according to the *Note on the Resettlement and Rehabilitation of Pong Dam Oustees in Rajasthan Canal Project Area*, a total of 339 *tikkas* were submerged by the Pong reservoir. Of these, 223 *tikkas* were fully submerged while 116 were partially affected.

The Union Government asked the Rajasthan government to shoulder the responsibility of rehabilitating the oustees on account of it being the chief beneficiary state. However, almost 28 years after their displacement, the majority of the Pong dam oustees continue to be condemned to a homeless existence with the promised land still eluding them. They find themselves being methodically hunted out of their houses and lands by the local people in Rajasthan while the Rajasthan government frowns upon them as encroachers or trespassers. The Himachal government, on its part, ignored its responsibility until it became too late to effectively intervene on behalf òf the oustees. The Himachalee has no one to look after him, neither his home government nor his host government. He is truly *aniket*, the homeless one.

The displaced population was to be rehabilitated in the command area of the Pong dam which is in Rajasthan. However, not all the oustees were rehabilitated there. Those who were not entitled to land compensation did not go to Rajasthan. Many among those who had gone to Rajasthan were also compelled to return to Himachal Pradesh. When our team met the officials at the resettlement and rehabilitation (R & R) office in Bikaner, Rajasthan, and asked for the list of rehabilitation sites, we were told that no comprehensive list or map indicating the settlements was available. But the government had reserved land in Anupgarh, Gharsana and Suratgarh in Ganganagar district, Vijaynagar, Raisingh Nagar and Chattargarh I and II. The names of resettlement colonies are based on the names of the nearest minor canal in the region.

Our team also went to R & R offices in Himachal Pradesh where we were told that the oustees in Rajasthan were rehabilitated in Anupgarh, Suratgarh, Gharsana, Vijaynagar, Khajuwala, Raisingh Nagar, Chattargarh I and II, Charanwala, Nachna, Puggal, Narwana and Jaisser. Those oustees who had settled themselves in Himachal Pradesh were now living in different areas depending upon their convenience.

TABLE 5.1
Some Resettlement Sites in Rajasthan

Colony	Name of Land	Tehsil	District
6P	Phogawali Canal	Anupgarh	Ganganagar
20P	Phogawali Canal	Anupgarh	Ganganagar
23P	Phogawali Canal	Anupgarh	Ganganagar
24P	Phogawali Canal	Anupgarh	Ganganagar
25P	Phogawali Canal	Anupgarh	Ganganagar
14K	Karmori Canal	Anupgarh	Ganganagar
12H	Hishamki Canal	Anupgarh	Ganganagar
20H	Hishamki Canal	Anupgarh	Ganganagar
66H	Hishamki Canal	Anupgarh	Ganganagar
3JKM	No information	Raisingh Nagar	Ganganagar
9BGD	No information	Raisingh Nagar	Ganganagar
3FDM	No information	Vijaynagar	Ganganagar
7BGD	No information	Vijaynagar	Ganganagar
4FDM	No information	Suratgarh	Ganganagar
2MD	Mamawadi	Gharsana	Ganganagar
3MD	Mamawadi	Gharsana	Ganganagar
4MD	Mamawadi	Gharsana	Ganganagar
1SM	Sakhi Minor	Gharsana	Ganganagar

No information was available on the names of colonies from *tehsils* Nachna, Charanwala in Jaisalmer district, Jaisser, Narwana, Puggal, Khajuwala and Chattargarh.

TABLE 5.2
Some Resettlement Sites in Himachal Pradesh

Name of Village	District
Bilaspur	Kangra
Nagrota Suriyan	Kangra
Sukhanara	Kangra
Bangoli	Kangra
Indira Colony	Kangra
Nurpur	Kangra
Dharamsala	Kangra

The list of the rehabilitation sites is not complete as neither the offices in Rajasthan nor those in Himachal Pradesh have maintained a list of the settlements. Based on the meagre information available, the team decided to visit oustees living in both the states. In

Rajasthan, we visited the colonies in Anupgarh. In Himachal Pradesh, we visited Bilaspur, Nagrota Suriyan, Sukhnara, Bangoli and Indira Colony.

Profile of the Displaced

The submergence zone, a part of Kangra district, was a beautiful green valley. It was officially recognised as the 'Haldoon Valley', i.e., the granary of Kangra. It was a region with rich and fertile land and an abundance of water resources.

Hardly any official information was available about the social life of its people in the pre-submergence period. The team had therefore to depend upon the oustees who drew us a rough sketch. They told us that the affected people belonged to different caste groups: Brahmins, Rajputs, Choudharys or Ghrits, Jats, Mahajans and the lower castes. There was a clear-cut distinction between the upper and lower caste groups as they lived separately in small clusters in their villages.

The people were mainly dependent on land. The majority were marginal farmers. According to an official source, each family jointly held an average landholding of 1 to 2 acres. As their holdings were small, they were also engaged in sharecropping or were tenants on others' lands. A few people who belonged to the upper castes had large holdings. There were some like the Mahajans who had small shops or were petty businessmen. According to the same source, the landless, constituting 2 per cent of the displaced population, were village artisans or agricultural labourers.[3] Some of the oustees had joined the armed forces, mainly in the lower ranks. There were a few professionals like teachers, doctors and lawyers as well.

The oustees informed us that there used to be schools in some of the submerged villages. But the literacy rate was below average. Quite a few villages were connected by bus and this was not the only facility provided. Very few of them were, however, electrified.

This information is not necessarily objectively correct as the past

---

[3] This information was collected from various government sources on the condition that they remained undisclosed.

always tends to look rosy, especially when the present is dismal and the future hopeless. It was not possible to substantiate this information as no socio-economic survey of the submergence area was undertaken and no official records for the same were available.

Awareness About the Project

Word about the project got around when the then Prime Minister, Pandit Jawaharlal Nehru, laid the foundation stone in 1960. This event had been given coverage by the local newspapers and All India Radio. But for many people, especially in the interior villages, the media had little impact. The land acquisition proceedings began in 1961. It was then that people realised that a dam was going to be built. Many of them, however, still remained unaware of the dam and with reason. One of the shortcomings of the Land Acquisition Act, 1894, is that the notification declared under it has to be published in the government gazette and two regional newspapers. To the illiterate population in India, the written word has no meaning and even the literate find it hard to gain access to the official gazette and newspapers in interior areas.

Though the project work had begun by 1961, little effort was made to impart any information about the different processes of the project. Even the educated oustees who had more information about the project than perhaps their less fortunate counterparts, had little information pertaining to the extent of submergence, or the compensation to be awarded.

The educated oustees, and those who had jobs outside their villages, admitted that the government had informed those affected in some areas about the time of submergence. The project officials, in the course of their conversation with our team, claimed that they had intimated the affected villagers about the time of submergence. They said that the officials had visited some villages in order to persuade people to shift before the waters were released. But they also admitted that many villages were left out, especially those in the interior areas, and people had, therefore, remained uninformed. However, while the government did not do its duty, the educated and the aware among the oustees were not completely blameless either.

The oustees told the team that Mr Pratap Singh Kairon, the late Chief Minister of Punjab had held a series of public meetings and had promised liberal compensation and rehabilitation to the oustees so that they would, in fact, be better off after their displacement. He had promised to personally supervise the entire process of resettlement. The people felt that had he still been alive the situation would not have been as bad.

Other political leaders made false promises to the effect that the oustees would be given spacious cemented houses with all infra-structural facilities. They were also promised 31 acres of land per landholder in Rajasthan. Those who did not want to go to Rajasthan were promised similar compensation in Himachal Pradesh. In this connection, the then Finance Minister, Mr Morarji Desai, during a visit to the submergence area, made several promises at a public meeting. In conclusion, he said, 'We will request you to move from your houses after the dam comes up. If you move, it will be good, otherwise we shall release the waters and drown you all'. Whether intentional or not, this statement turned out to be a forewarning.

As matters stood, the affected people did not believe that the project authorities would actually release the waters before they had moved from their houses. The situation was made worse because the local political leaders told the oustees that they did not need to move from their homes and that they would ensure that water was not released. Many people had been lulled into believing that the government would not release the waters as long as they were living there. This resulted in heavy losses to the oustees and when the waters were finally released, many were taken unawares. They had to flee their homes, leaving behind their belongings. Sumernath Sharma, an advocate and an oustee settled in Dharam-sala, HP, said that some villages were washed away causing several deaths. Two villages, Paroka and Kalyanvadi, which were close to his own village, were among these.

Compensation and Rehabilitation

As mentioned earlier, to begin with, only three states, Punjab, Rajasthan and Haryana, were involved in the project. The formation of Himachal Pradesh in 1966 complicated the situation.

The HP government entered the picture only in 1967. By this time, the processes regarding acquisition of land and the basic plans for rehabilitation were well under way. At this stage, the administrative control of the project was transferred to the Union Government through the Beas Board. As a result, all problems relating to displacement and rehabilitation that arose when the state came into being had to be taken up at the ministerial level This was obviously a time-consuming process and the decisions to be taken depended on the political leanings of the different parties that ruled the states.

The Himachal government was confronted with another problem. Before the reorganisation of states, the Punjab government had made some promises to the oustees concerning resettlement. In the new state, the expectations of the affected persons continued to be the same but the HP government found itself unable to fulfil many of them due to their status in the project.

A detailed study of the resettlement and rehabilitation plans reveals that there were no clear-cut guidelines or policies for either calculating cash compensation or for resettlement of the oustees, which were undertaken on the basis of various recommendations made by committees from time to time.

CASH COMPENSATION

The landholders were entitled to cash compensation for land, houses and trees. But the landless, the encroachers and the artisans were to be compensated only for houses and trees. All oustees had a share in the amount that was to be paid for common property resources (CPR).

The cut-off date for calculating cash compensation was 31 March 1961, the date of publication of Section 4 under the Land Acquisition Act, 1894. According to the article, 'Rehabilitation of Displaced Persons at Beas Dam Project', dated 1987, the land was graded into eight categories in order to determine the cash award. Each category was evaluated accordingly. The rate of compensation awarded for the highest class of land, i.e., *Nehri-do-fasli* (irrigated yielding two crops) was Rs 140 per *kanal*[4] in 1962–63, and others in

---

[4] *Kanal* is a unit of land measurement in Punjab and Himachal Pradesh. 1 acre = 9.7 *Kanals*.

downward ratio. There was no information available about the rates paid for the other categories of land.

The rates at which compensation was paid turned out to be even lower. Kishore Chand from Indira Colony in HP said. 'I was paid Rs 135 per *kanal* for the best irrigated land.'

Dissatisfied with the award, the oustees appealed to the Deputy Commissioner who increased the award for the best grade of land in 1965 to Rs 650. But this too was not accepted by the oustees and they continued to agitate. Seven hundred and forty-three appellants filed applications before the district judge who enhanced the compensation rate to Rs 1,000 per *kanal*. But the Union of India felt that this rate was too high and appealed before the High Court for a lower rate. The High Court, however, maintained the earlier award of Rs 1,000 per *kanal*.

In 1979, the Union Government appealed to the Supreme Court in the matter of the 743 cases. In 1983, the Court decided to lower the rate to Rs 750 per *kanal*. This created further complications. Most oustees had already received the enhanced amount against a surety. The Union of India now decided to recover the differential amount of Rs 250 from each oustee.

Repeated appeals were made by the oustees. In a North Zonal meeting held in October 1985, the HP government in consultation with the three states concerned decided to waive recovery of the differential amount. This decision was not applicable to the 743 cases decided by the Supreme Court. It was, however, clarified that in the case of those who had already withdrawn the money and were too poor to repay it, the state government would refund the amount.

The oustees who were to receive the revised amount of compensation were entitled to interest and solatium at the enhanced rate. For this, about 20,336 applications were received by the Land Acquisition Officer, Beas Dam Talwara, for redetermination of the compensation. Only 703 cases had been decided by June 1989 (Minutes of the District level Pong Dam Oustees Rehabilitation Advisory Committee Meeting held under the Chairmanship of the Revenue Minister, on 19 June 1989).

The ongoing litigation for a just compensation, spanning a long period of time, was both complicated and confusing for most oustees. As Jaisi Ram Khatta, now settled in village Bilaspur of

HP, very aptly pointed out, 'Only highly educated oustees whose number was quite small were aware about the legal procedure. Most of us did not know what was happening.' He added, 'I cannot even read and write. I have never been involved in any court matters. How was I to know what to do? I did just what I was told or what the others were doing.'

Due to constant revisions of compensation rates from 1962 to 1983, the oustees were being paid at varying rates. Kishan Chand, now settled in Sukhnara village of HP, said, 'After 1965 compensation was paid at so many different rates that many of us had no knowledge about the basis on which the compensation was being awarded to us. We just did what the officials instructed us to do.'

Mangal Das, settled in village Bilaspur (HP), told us that he had received Rs 650 per *kanal* for his two plots which belonged to two different categories of land, i.e., best irrigated and irrigable. On the other hand, Ramesh Chand from village Bangoli (HP), received Rs 650 for his irrigable plot of land.

It is a fact that many people like Mangal Das and Ramesh Chand did get compensation at different rates for the same category of land. At the same time, it cannot be ruled out that they could have been ignorant of the repeated revisions of the award and, therefore, continued to feel that they were being discriminated against.

The claims for receiving the cash amount had to be filed within a stipulated period after each award. As a result, the majority missed out on the opportunity to file their claims within the required period. This happened despite a declaration published by the Himachal government, an indication of how ineffective this method of communication is. With no permanent place of domicile, the oustees had by then dispersed to different places. Kishan Chand, presently settled in Sukhnara (HP) echoed the feelings of 12 other oustees taking part in the meeting when he said, 'Once again, we had to go through the whole process of filing another application, thereby wasting our time and money. Many of us had to even take loans owing to this delay'. Pointing towards the cluster of the tiny one-room mud houses with roofs almost caving in, he said, 'Perhaps you can understand our suffering better by seeing for yourself. My family lived in a bigger three room house earlier'

Another problem faced by the oustees related to the withdrawal of the enhanced amount of compensation from the High Court. They were required to furnish individual bank guarantees for the same.

N.C. Ram was once a landholder but, at present, earns his livelihood as a landless labourer in HP. Referring to the protracted proceedings for higher compensation, which took up all their scarce resources, he said, 'In spite of having fought for so long to get our entitlements, we have still not received the arrears. Though they belong to us legally, we cannot withdraw the amount until we have furnished individual guarantees. We do not own property in HP anymore, so how can we comply with the Court's orders for a guarantee? Besides, this will mean several visits to the Court, which, in turn, will mean losing out on our daily wages'. He went on to say, 'We are fed up of all this. We can see no end to these problems. What is the point of getting the money when I will not be alive anymore and my family will have broken up in the mean-time?'

It was as recently as May 1989 that at a meeting of the State Level Pong Dam Oustees Rehabilitation Advisory Committee a final decision was taken according to which the state of HP would stand as a guarantor for all the oustees to enable them to get the entitled amount.

Mr Randhawa of PDOA told us that apart from the compensation received for houses, land and trees, the oustees were also to be given approximately 5 crores on account of common property resources (CPR). This was confirmed by the R & R official in Dharamsala during the team's visit. This amount was to be distri-buted to the panchayats who were to give the oustees their share. But none of the oustees had been paid their share of the money allocated for CPR.

Mr Randhawa also told the team that when the matter was raised with the government officials, they informed him that they could not disburse the amount as the panchayats had broken up following displacement. He added that when the issue was once again raised at a high level meeting at Manali (HP), the govern-ment had decided to directly distribute the amount amongst the oustees. But this decision too was not carried out.

In reply to our question, an R & R official at Dharamsala told us that it was not possible to locate all the oustees. Further, since many of them had settled in HP, the state government had decided to use the amount for developmental works in the mini-revenue settlements. However, we could not check if this money was actually being utilised for that purpose, due to the non-availability of any records.

RESETTLEMENT AND REHABILITATION

A Committee comprising the Chief Ministers (CMs) of all the three states concerned, Rajasthan, Punjab and Haryana was constituted by the central government to suggest a plan for rehabilitation. They met for the first time in August 1961. Subsequently, the Chief Minister of HP also became a member of the Committee. The Committee met six times between August 1961 and July 1968 and discussed various aspects concerning the eligibility criteria, number of oustees, process of resettlement, etc., of the Pong dam oustees.

In 1969, the HP government forwarded a list to the Committee, declaring a total of 20,722 families as oustees. The Rajasthan government demanded a verification of this figure. They found a number of discrepancies. The list included some major sons, i.e., above 18, who were not landowners. Also, some outsiders who had land in the Pong dam area figured on the list. This led to a dispute on the eligibility of oustees for allotment of land for resettlement. Finally, both governments came to an agreement on eligibility criteria. Accordingly, only 16,100 families were found eligible for land compensation in Rajasthan.

Appreciating the 'hardships and sacrifices made by the Pong dam oustees', the Committee admitted that 'the oustees must be treated as a special class of allottees and the allotment of land must provide them with the means of a regular occupation' (Note on Resettlement and Rehabilitation of Pong Dam Oustees Rajasthan Canal Project Area, undated). The Committee laid down that each landowner-oustee, irrespective of the quantum of land submerged, would be entitled to allotment of one *murabba* which is the equivalent of 15.625 acres of irrigated land, in the Rajasthan Canal Area on 20 annual instalments. The cost was to be the same as was being charged from the local landless who were being allotted land by the Rajasthan government.

This Committee also agreed that the basis of allotment of land for resettlement had to be ownership of the land submerged. The members were very specific in this regard. In December 1968, it was decided that artisans, landless labourers, tenants, etc., would be given only house plots within the *abadi* areas. But the oustees would have to pay for the houses that were to be constructed by the government. They were, however, not entitled to any agricultural land. The Rajasthan colonisation department on its part was expected to provide housing, roads, water supply, etc.

These decisions, along with other guidelines emerging out of the meetings of the Committee were published on 16 September 1972 in the form of Colonisation (Allotment of Government Land to Pong Dam Oustees in Rajasthan Canal Colony) Rules (henceforth referred to as the Colonisation Rules). The state government had framed these Rules according to the Rajasthan Colonisation Act, 1954. They were enforced with effect from 11 April 1973.

While the discussions of the Committee were still underway, and the Rules were still to be finalised, two groups of oustees had already been shifted to Rajasthan beginning in 1965-66. By 1972, when the Colonisation Rules were finalised, a major part of the submergence zone had already been acquired and most of the oustee families had been displaced.

The Colonisation Rules

I. ELIGIBILITY FOR LAND COMPENSATION

1. The Rajasthan government had to reserve land in specific areas falling under the command area of the Rajasthan Canal for allotment to oustees. Allotment of land to oustees under the Colonisation Rules was to be done from this reserved land only [Rule 3 (i)].
2. The Colonisation Rules defined an 'oustee' as a person who had been a permanent and continuous resident of the Pong reservoir area from, on, or before 31 March 1961, and had been paid cash for land acquired for the dam [Rule 2 (ix)].
3. In order to be eligible for allotment of land in Rajasthan, a landowner with less than 20 acres (held either severally or jointly) had to lose 30 per cent or more of his holding while an oustee with more than 20 acres (held severally or jointly) had to lose 50 per cent or more of his holding [Rule 2 (ix)].

4. In case of a joint holding, all co-sharers were to be considered as one oustee and allotted one unit of land, i.e., 15.625 acres [Rule 4 (3)].
5. The next clause goes on to add that only those oustees would be eligible for land whose names appeared in one particular *khewat*[5] in the *Jamabandi*[6] (revenue record of a village unit) up to 1961 and thereafter up to the time of acquisition [Rule 4 (iv)]. Such an oustee would need to prove that he had been assessed and had paid land revenue separately and regularly up to 1961 and thereafter until the date of its acquisition [Rule 4 (i)a].
6. After 1961, only ownership through succession was recognised. All legal successors were to be considered as one oustee eligible for allotment of one unit of *murabba* only [Rule 4 (iii)].

II. PROCEDURE FOR ALLOTMENT

1. The eligible oustee was required to procure a certificate and identity card from the HP government as proof of being an oustee. Within two months of these being issued, he had to personally file an application in the office of the allotting authority to be provisionally registered until he was given clearance by the Rajasthan government [Rule 5 (i), (ii) and (iii)].
2. Following the provisional registration of such an oustee and a lengthy scrutiny of legitimacy of the oustee concerned, the final decision of the allotting authority was to be conveyed to him [Rules 4, 5 and 6].
3. Once the application was cleared and the allotment order in the reserved land granted, the allottee had to take possession within 45 days of the receipt of the notice for allotment [Rule 5 (vi)].
4. The same was to be considered cancelled in case the allottee failed to take possession within the specified 45 days [Rule 5 (vii)].

III. TERMS AND CONDITIONS GOVERNING ALLOTMENT

1. No oustee was to be vested with ownership (*khatedari*) rights

---

[5] *Khewat Khata* is the record of each holding (or *khewat*) in a *tikka*.
[6] *Jamabandi* is the revenue record mentioning the details of *Khewat Khatas* of a village.

till the expiry of 20 years after allotment and till the payment of the full cost of land and any other dues [Rule 6 (iii)].

2. The sale or transference of land in any manner whatsoever was forbidden even if it be alienation of land in the form of *noker-nama* or *mukhtiarnama* [Rule 6 (iv)].

3. Within two months of allotment, it was compulsory on the part of the ousted allottee to start living permanently in the *chak abadi* [(rehabilitation centre) Rule 6 (v)] and cultivate the land personally, i.e., by means of 'one's own labour or the labour of any one member of the family' [Rule 6 (vi)].

4. The entire land had to be 'brought under plough' within a period of six months from the date of allotment [Rule 6 (viii)].

5. The presence of the allottee himself on his land, especially at the time of field inspection, i.e., *girdawari*, was compulsory . He was required to produce his identity card as and when demanded by the colonisation or revenue authorities [Rule 6 (ix)].

6. The price for the best quality land to be given out of the reserved land in the command area was fixed at Rs 20,000 per *murabba* [Rule 7], and possession for the land was to be handed over only after the payment of the initial instalment within 45 days from the day of allotment. This was to be paid in 20 annual instalments [Rule 7 (v)].

   For the Johad paitan land, the price to be paid was fixed at double that of the cost of Nali land [Rule 7 (ii)].

   It was also specified that in case the land was developed by the state government, the price would also include the expenditure on developing it. The oustee was also required to pay 6 per cent interest on the amount spent on developing the land [Rule 7 (v)].

7. In case a of breach of any of the above conditions, the allotment was liable to be cancelled with immediate effect and the land was to revert to the state government for fresh allotment [Rule 8].

The approach and attitude of the project authorities towards the issue of rehabilitation of oustees is clearly evident from all the official documents, particularly those concerning discussions at the Committee meetings. During the series of meetings, all members of the Committee comprising representatives of the three states concerned and the Union Government, defined rehabilitation of oustees as 'an ex-gratia voluntary act agreed between the Rajasthan and Himachal Governments'. This was reiterated by the Cabinet Secretary to the Government of India in his statement in the Award of July 1972. 'I [Cabinet Secretary] would wish to emphasise that this is an unique case of Land Acquisition Oustees being rehabilitated in a state different from the one in which the land is acquired. There can be no rules and regulations in regard to such an *ad hoc* arrangement. The matter can be governed purely by goodwill between the Reservoir-land-Donor State and the Irrigation-beneficiary-State and by humanitarian considerations' (Note on Resettlement and Rehabilitation of Pong Dam Oustees in Rajasthan Canal Project Area, 1987).

In accordance with the Committee's decision, 2.25 lakh acres was to be reserved for the oustees. The Colonisation Rules had laid down that 'The state government may reserve land in specific command areas of Rajasthan Canal for allotment to Pong Dam Oustees and the allotment under these Rules shall be made out of this land only. The allotment authority shall prepare a list or lists of such reserved land in Form I.' However, the Rajasthan government did not reserve the specified 2.25 lakh acres of land in the command area before the displacement of all the oustees in 1972–73. Instead, they identified and reserved land in two phases. These corresponded to the phases in which allotments were made. The first phase stretched from 1966 to 1982 and the second phase began in 1982.

According to a report by the Additional Colonisation Commissioner, Bikaner dated 2 September 1989, the allotment authority had, at first, reserved only 1,62,000 acres in the command area. A total of 44,325 *bighas*[7] was later reserved in Charanwala in Jaisalmer district. Of this, only 20,210 *bighas* was command land. The remaining 63,000 acres is yet to be identified and reserved by the Colonisation Department of Rajasthan.

Although the government had reserved land exclusively for allotment to oustees, a large part of this land was used for purposes other than allotment. Thus, a total of 13,879 acres out of the reserved land was for forests, for the use of the local landless, and the Border Security Force. A part of it was also auctioned to the

[7] *Bigha* is a unit of land measurement.

local population (Report of the Additional Colonisation Commission, Bikaner, dated 2 September 1989). Therefore, in reality, more than 63,000 acres of land for the oustees needs to be identified.

In reply to the question raised in the Lok Sabha on 16 May 1985 and again on 17 April 1990, regarding the reservation of 2.25 lakh acres of land, the Ministers in charge had claimed that this total had been earmarked by 1970. These replies stand in total contradiction to the facts stated in the above report.

The land reserved for allotment to the oustees was of three categories and they were required to pay for the allotted land.

TABLE 5.3

Soil category	Price per square of 15.625 acres
Nali	Rs 20,000
Light loam	Rs 16,875
Sandy loam	Rs 12,600

The price of Johad Paitan land was double that of Nali land, i.e, Rs 40,000 per square of 15.625 acres.

It was also specified that if the allotted land had been developed by the government, the cost of the land would include the amount spent towards its development together with a 6 per cent interest on the cost of development. The total cost of the land was to be recovered in 20 years.

While talking to government officials of Himachal Pradesh, we were informed that the Rajasthan government had enhanced the cost of each *murabba* of Nali land to Rs 29,000 in 1981. This was further raised to Rs 35,000 in 1983. They added, 'the current market rate of the *murabba* has gone up to Rs 4 to 5 lakhs. In areas where the irrigation facility has reached, land has become a lucrative asset. That is why the Rajasthan authorities are reluctant to allot irrigated land in the reserved area. Instead, they prefer to auction it.' In reply to another question, the team was told that the Himachal government was not aware if the Rajasthan authorities had issued any circulars to officially declare their decisions regarding land prices.

When this was checked with the Rajasthan officials, they admitted that the rates were enhanced and said: 'We did reserve land for the oustees. But with irrigation, the value of the land has shot up. Why should we allot this land to the oustees at subsidised rates?'

Actual Allotment

The allotment of land was to be made under the Colonisation Rules. These Rules, as mentioned, had been published in the government gazette which was inaccessible to the people at large. As such, most oustees remained in the dark about the Rules. That was not all. The process of allotment under the rules proved to be lengthy and complicated.

The authorities had not specified the period for the rehabilitation of the oustees. All the oustees had been displaced by 1972–73. During the transitory period, no arrangements had been made for them in Rajasthan. This became an additional problem for their resettlement. Since the majority of the oustees had dispersed in small groups, village units broke up. This made it even more difficult for the people to exchange information.

The eligibility criteria for allotment did not separately recognise all co-sharers of one *khewat khata*. In many cases, co-sharers were from different families or from different caste groups (Resettlement and Rehabilitation of Pong Dam Oustees in Rajasthan Canal Area, undated). Therefore, one wonders what criteria had been used by the Rajasthan government to select the oustees from each *khewat khata* for allotment of land. Mangal Das, who had lost his entire holding of 12 *kanals* of land is now settled in Bilaspur in HP along with 12 other families who also lost their lands. He said, 'All of us lost our total lands. We had applied for allotment but we did not receive it. Nobody gave us any information as to why we were not given land.' At Sukhnara village in HP, we met Kishan Chand who had settled there with 30 to 35 families after they had received cash compensation for their submerged lands. They too were ignorant about why they did not receive any land compensation. There were others who were similarly placed. It could be because these oustees were co-sharers of a particular *khewat khata* and the stringent rules for eligibility for land compensation had left them with nothing. As a result, only 16,100 families were found eligible for land compensation in Rajasthan. Of these, 9,195 oustees had been allotted land in Rajasthan by 1982, i.e., during the first phase.

Details of year-wise allotments made:

TABLE 5.4

Year	No. of allotments
1966-72	572
1973-74	8,389
1976	12
1977	32
1978	101
1979	63
1982	26
16 years	9,195

Source: Note on Resettlement and Rehabilitation of the Pong Dam Oustees in the Rajasthan Canal Project Area, undated.

Out of the 9,195 allotments made during the first phase, 6,601 allotments were cancelled. These cancellations were effected due to various reasons. The largest number of allotments in 3,415 cases were cancelled because of their inability to pay the instalments on the due date [Rule 5 (vii)]. Another 2,302 allottees lost their lands for not having taken possession of their *murabbas* within the stipulated 45 days of the receipt of their allotment order [Rule 5 (vii)]. Subletting of land, which was treated by the authorities as *benami* transactions, led to cancellations in 689 cases [Rule 6 (iv)]. Their inability to cultivate the land themselves, which was to commence within six months of allotment, resulted in 195 cancellations [Rules 6 (vi) and 7] (Note on Resettlement and Rehabilitation of Pong Dam Oustees in Rajasthan Canal Project Area, undated).

The Himachal government (Note on Resettlement and Rehabilitation of Pong Dam Oustees in the Rajasthan Canal Project Area dated 1987) accepted that the rules that were framed to facilitate the work related to resettlement and rehabilitation, had, in reality, worked against the interests of the Pong dam oustees. Thus, by 1982, although 9,195 oustees had been made allotments, only 2,594 could retain their lands.

Sohni Devi who was allotted land in *chak* 4 JM of Anupgarh

tehsil told us, 'I had been cultivating my land from 1973 to 1977. But when I fell ill, I had to go to my relatives in Kangra for my treatment due to lack of medical facilities in Rajasthan. On my return, I found my *murabba* cancelled.' Sohni Devi was not the only one whose allotment was cancelled for not being physically present on the *murabba*. The reasons for absence from the land obviously did not carry much weight with the authorities, no matter how grave the cause.

Even in cases where the allottees were physically present, they could not retain their lands, mostly because they were unable to pay their instalments on time. Karam Chand, displaced in 1973, was allotted land in 1976. Though he was able to pay his first instalment, he had no money left from his compensation to pay for the second instalment in 1977, following which his *murabba* was cancelled. This was because the enhancement of the compensation amount had yet to be finally decided. What money he had was used up during the transitory phase and later to develop his land.

Quite clearly, the authorities did not view the cases of the oustees in the light of the factors that were responsible for their inability to abide by the rules. For them, blind implementation of the rules was what mattered most.

Of the 16,100 families found eligible for allotment, 9,195 oustees had been made allotments. According to the officials at the R & R office in HP, the remaining oustees had not applied within the stipulated 60 days from the day of receiving cash compensation [Rule 8 (iii)].

Some of them did not apply because they were initially unwilling to go to Rajasthan. As K.K. Pathania, now settled in village Gharsana, Rajasthan, said, 'For us, it was like being forced to live in a place which was out of [the] bounds of civilisation.' For this and other reasons, the majority of the oustees we met in Rajasthan and HP had not at first been prepared to settle in Rajasthan until they realised that they could not continue to live in HP without any source of livelihood. Kishorilal from Anupgarh, Rajasthan, rightly pointed out, 'For the majority of oustees like myself who were left with no means of livelihood, the prospect of settling in Rajasthan was the only alternative offering hope of some stability in life. We accepted resettlement in Rajasthan because of the continued promises of proper rehabilitation being made by both governments '

Thus, at the end of the first phase, as only 2,594 families were able to retain their land, as many as 13,506 families remained to be allotted land.

Appeals for Reallotment

The 6,601 oustees whose allotments were cancelled made repeated appeals before both the Rajasthan and Himachal governments. The members of the Pong Dam Oustees Association (PDOA) in Delhi (themselves oustees) also submitted various memorandums to both governments and met a number of politicians and concerned government officials at the centre and state. The HP government took up the matter with the Rajasthan government at the state level as well as with· the centre. At a meeting held in September 1981 the Chief Ministers of Himachal Pradesh and Rajasthan decided to amend certain clauses of the Colonisation Rules. A 'Memorandum of Understanding' was signed on 13 September 1981 which incorporated the decisions taken at the meeting to amend the Rules. These amendments were published in a notification on 22 April 1982.

Amendments

According to the amendments, the oustees could now cultivate the land through an agent/manager. The period for taking possession of land was extended to 90 days. The period for cultivating the entire holding was also extended to three years, 50 per cent of the land was meant to be irrigated in the first year, and of the remaining 50 per cent, half was to be irrigated during the second year and the rest in the third year. Any default in payment of instalments was rescheduled with 6 per cent interest. Under the new Rules, the oustees could live on the *murabba* itself instead of *chak abadi*.

The period for acquiring the proprietary rights to the allotted land was reduced from 20 to 10 years, provided all payable dues had been deposited by this time. But the right to sell was still to be conferred on the *khatedar* (legal landholder) after the expiry of 20 years.

In some cases, land was allotted where irrigation facilities had not yet reached and the allotted land had been encroached by non-oustees. These issues were also taken up at the meeting. Following the amendments, the unirrigated allotted lands were to be exchanged for lands where irrigation had been made available. Further, the reallotment of land in cases where the cancelled lands were to be restored was to be done only after it had been freed of all encroachments.

The Memorandum of Understanding also declared that all cases of cancelled lands and those pending for fresh allotments would be reconsidered. However, the Committee took a serious view of the 689 oustees who had either sold or transferred their lands during the first phase in contravention of the Rules, i.e, those who were involved in *benami* transactions. It was decided not to review their cases for restoration. The amended Rules were once again published in the gazette in 1982.

Allotments under Phase II

Following the amendments, only 4,734 oustees came forward with applications for restoration of their cancelled *murabbas* and 1,814 oustees applied for fresh allotment.

According to a government report (Note on Resettlement and Rehabilitation of PDOS, dated 1987), '863 cases were arbitrarily rejected out of 4,734 cases up to April 1983.' Out of the 1,814 applications, the cases of 1,559 oustees were sent by the Chief Minister of HP to the Chief Minister of Rajasthan. The remaining 255 cases were rejected by the HP government on grounds of non-eligibility.

Till April 1983, allotments were restored in 3,349 cases. However, only 1,559 cases finally got possession. In the remaining cases, possession was unnecessarily delayed. During the process of review, the oustees were continuously harassed, with hearings adjourned more than four to five times. In the event that the applicant was unable to be present at any one hearing, his application was cancelled forthwith.

Devraj is a tailor settled at present in Indira Colony in HP. He told our team that he had been allotted land outside the command area which he rejected. He had then filed an application with the allotment authority, Bikaner, for restoration of land in the command area. 'I was frequently called for hearings at the Bikaner office. For every hearing, I had to leave my work for more than a week and incur a lot of expenditure. My income is meagre as it is.' Since his compensation amount had been exhausted, it became difficult for him to pursue his case. He added, 'I could not go for one of the hearings. Later, when I went to the office, I was told that my application had been rejected. I have lost all hope of getting any land. I lost even what little money I had.'

Despite the amendments in 1982, the cancellations continued and the oustees' problems remained. This was so because although most clauses of the Rules were amended, they had merely touched upon the fringe of the problem. Nothing was done to ease the adverse living conditions which had been a major deterrent in their resettlement. Above all, the unrelenting attitude of the officials also remained unchanged so that the allotments continued to be cancelled at the slightest pretext. Hence, their difficulties, as earlier, included allotment of encroached land or land in areas other than the command area, law and order, lack of civic amenities, and so on.

Once again, cancellations due to the problems faced by the oustees were discussed at a ministerial level meeting held in Jaipur on 15 June 1983. Following discussions, the Rajasthan government agreed to further amend the amended Rules of 1982. The decisions taken during this meeting were confirmed at the Chief Ministers' meeting held at Udaipur on 6 February 1984, and were incorporated as amended Rules from 22 October 1984.

According to these Rules, the cancelled allotments were to be restored to the oustees provided *a* they were residing within the *chak abadi*; *b* they had already taken possession of the allotted land before it was cancelled or; *c* they had not been able to take possession due to non-payment of the first instalment within the stipulated time. It was also decided that all the rejected cases would be reviewed. The non-command/unirrigated lands were to be exchanged for command/irrigated lands. The new Rules emphasised that only land free of encroachments was to be allotted in the cases of both fresh applicants and those applying for restoration of cancelled land.

Subsequent to the 1982 amendments, the 863 cases that had

been rejected were now to be taken up for review. Up to June 1985, under phase II, a total of 4,734 applications were received for review of cancelled allotments and 1,559 for fresh allotments. However, of the 4,734 review cases, possession was delivered in only 2,302 cases. The rest of the cases were pending under various heads—encroachments; exchange of non-command/unirrigated lands for command/irrigated lands; disputed cases of double allotments; cases under stay order, etc.

As matters stood, from 1966 to 1985, only 4,896 families of the 16,100 eligible oustees were able to actually get possession of land: 2,594 in the first phase and 2,302 in the second phase.

Sohni Devi, whose allotment had been cancelled during the first phase, was reallotted land in Anupgarh in the second phase. Having paid the first instalment and other dues when she went to take possession of the land, she found it illegally occupied by a non-oustee who claimed that it had been allotted to him. She informed the Colonisation Commissioner but till 1989 no action had been taken.

Karam Chand's allotment was also cancelled. His land was restored to him after the 1982 amendments. But he could not take possession within the specified 90 days due to non-payment of the first instalment. On reapplying in 1985, he paid his first instalment on time, along with Rs 3,600 which was the 6 per cent interest for default of payment. But he still did not get possession of his land. During this period, both his parents expired while he was forced to earn his living as a landless agricultural labourer. He told our team, 'If I had to remain without land, I could have used all the money that I spent on land for some small business. I know now for sure that I will never get land and I have lost my money as well. Is the Rajasthan government so badly off that they have to cheat poor people like us of our hard-earned money ?'

Many others like Sohni Devi and Karam Chand who were allotted land either in the first or the second phase found their allotments cancelled for one reason or the other.

Thus, the facility of reapplying for restoration or fresh allotments did not really help the oustees. Even in cases where the oustees did manage to get the allotment order, they could not gain possession of their land.

Though the Colonisation Rules of 1972 and the two amendments in 1982 and 1984 had repeatedly emphasised that the oustees must be allotted irrigated land within the command area, the reality was quite the contrary. All the allotments were given in an area which was out of the command zone. Furthermore, the majority of the allotments were in areas adjacent to the Indo-Pak border (Note on Resettlement and Rehabilitation of PDOS in the Rajasthan Canal Area, undated).

A total of 44,325 *bighas* in 44 *chaks* was reserved in Charanwala in Nachna *tehsil* of Jaisalmer district. Of this, 20,210 *bighas* was command land while the remaining 24,115 *bighas* was outside the command area. A total of 1,882 allotments were made in this area, but the oustees were unwilling to take possession of their allotted lands as no irrigation facility and, more importantly, no drinking water was available. The oustees appealed to the HP government. Once again, the Himachal Chief Minister took up the matter with the Chief Minister of Rajasthan.

The two governments finally decided that possession could not be delivered until irrigation facilities had reached the resettlement sites in Charanwala. However, the Rajasthan authorities did not abide by this agreement and issued notices of allotment directly to the oustees instead of through the office of the DC (R & R) at Talwara. This notice warned the oustees that their allotments would be cancelled if they did not take possession within the time limit. By the time the DC's office was intimated of this and could take suitable action, 137 oustees, fearing cancellation of their allotments, had already deposited their first instalments and 115 had taken possession. But most other oustees maintained that unless drinking water was provided they would not move into an area which was a virtual desert. When our team talked to the Rajasthan officials they said, 'This facility would be given only after the oustees started living there. After all, we would be spending a lot of money to lay down water pipes, etc. We want to make sure that there are people at the other end who will use the water.' The Rajasthan government had made separate rules for allotting land to their landless population. According to these, they could start paying the instalments for the *murabba* two years after water for irrigation had been made available. They were also entitled to free wheat rations for one year to initially help them tide over their economic difficulty. The HP government requested the Rajasthan government to extend similar benefits to the Pong dam oustees who were also allotted land in Charanwala. But the

Rajasthan government did not agree to do so and the stalemate continues to this day.

Despite repeated promises made by both governments, the oustees were continuously allotted non-command/unirrigated lands. The oustees resettled in Anupgarh were the first to receive water in 1975–76. But during this time, only the main canal reached the area while the distributary system was still to be completed. This meant that only those farmers who were in the vicinity of the main canal benefited.

The Canal Area Development Authority (CADA) conducted a survey of the command area and brought out a report (undated) based on their findings. One of their findings, quoted in the report of the On-the-Spot Evaluation team[8] submitted in July 1989, was that most of the allotted lands were either partially irrigated or totally unirrigated. But the local *patwari*, in his land records, had shown them as completely irrigated. As such, the oustees were made to pay the cost of irrigation facility for this land.

Ganga Ram was one such oustee who was allotted land in 21H where there was no sign of any irrigation facility. He told us that after 20 years of displacement, he had nothing to fall back upon as the land was unproductive. 'Before displacement, I had a 25–acre orchard in Himachal Pradesh. I was able to sustain my family reasonably well. But what have I got now? Nothing but a dry piece of land! The rules bind me to remain on the land or else I will lose even this. It feels like a frightening dream at the end of my life.'

Even where minor canals had been constructed, the oustees found it difficult to irrigate their fields. This was apparently because the area was uneven and undulating and the water level in the minor canals was considerably lower than the level of the fields. For instance, in the case of 55 *murabbas* of 16 GD and 18 GD colonies, water in the GD canal flowed 10 feet below the agricultural fields.

Not only were the minor canals technically faulty but the *khalas* (distributary channels) were no better. They sloped in such a manner that water flowed backwards to the mouth of the minor canal rather than towards the fields. Uttam Chand of Anupgarh

---

[8] To assess the problems of resettlement, the HP government in consultation with members of the PDOA decided (in May 1989) to form an on-the-spot evaluation study team. This team comprises the HP government officials as well as the members of the PDOA.

colony, pointing towards the *khala* passing through his plot of land, said, 'You can see everything for yourself. Not only is the slope faulty, it has even breached at several points.'

Aduram, a local resident of Anupgarh who tills the lands of many oustees in the area, showed our team the *khala* passing through one such field. 'Its embankment was washed away in January 1986, on the very first day when water was released.'

According to a government official the *khalas* were supposed to be cemented for which the government had taken a loan from the World Bank. The interest on the loan was to be recovered from each oustee, a sum amounting to Rs 7,000 to 9,000. Despite this, they had remained uncemented. Therefore, the *khalas* often breached and the oustees persistently complained about this problem. But no action was taken because the Rajasthan authorities responded with the contention that the *khalas* were the responsibility of the oustees. Another problem that continues to date. Thus, although 4,924 oustees were able to get possession of land, they did not really benefit because without irrigation their lands remained uncultivable and therefore economically unviable.

Out of the 16,100 families, 912 oustee families had sold or transferred their lands against the rules and 223 cases which had come up for review under phase II were rejected on eligibility criteria. Therefore, only 15,188 families finally remained to be rehabilitated in Rajasthan. Till 1989, many cases were still pending before the allotment authorities in Rajasthan.

TABLE 5.5

Pending for possession under phase I	992
Pending for various reasons under phase II (1982 onwards)	882
Pending cases for fresh allotments(phase II)	1,559
Under illegal encroachment	77
Exchange of non-command land for command land	61
Disputed cases of double allotment	10
Cases under stay order	49
Allotments made but cancellation due to Violation of Rules	84
Other cases, position not known	6
Pending for decision under Rule 8AA	29
Total	3,749

Source: Minutes of District Level Meeting at Dharamsala, HP, on 19 June 1989.

Oustees Settled in Himachal Pradesh

Due to the existing situation in Rajasthan, many oustees were forced to return to Himachal Pradesh. One such oustee, Jaisi Ram, who managed to purchase 8 to 10 *kanals* of land in Bilaspur village, said, 'The situation in Rajasthan is very bad and the government is doing nothing. I had not taken my family there due to lack of facilities. Finally, I too had to come back because of the law and order problem. Now I do not want to go to Rajasthan. I am living here peacefully.' Not all the oustees who returned to HP, however, were as lucky as Jaisi Ram.

Those landed oustees who were not found eligible for land compensation were forced to migrate in search of wage labour. Pramod Singh, whom we met in Bilaspur, was working at a road construction site. 'Now, I make baskets and sell them. I also work on daily wages wherever work is available. I have gone in search of work to Punjab, U P and even to Delhi. This dam has made us landless as well as homeless.'

Our team asked the R & R officials in Himachal if they had made any provisions for the oustees who were not entitled to land in Rajasthan. We were told that the oustees had approached them for some assistance. Following this in 1988, the government decided to allot up to 10 *bighas* of land to each oustee family and ordered a mini-revenue settlement to be formed. Approximately 5,059 oustee families were found to be entitled to land. The officials further informed us that this work was still in progress as the finalisation of the list of oustees from different villages was still underway. However, there were no official documents available to substantiate this decision of the government.

Law and Order

In 1973, Garib Dass, an oustee, was murdered in broad daylight in Anupgarh by anti-social elements. But the accused were not indicted by the Court. Two oustees were beaten up in *chak* 1 NRD in 1982 and permanently disabled (Note on Resettlement and Rehabilitation of Pong Dam Oustees in the Rajasthan Canal Project Area, undated).

Physical torture of oustees is a common feature. Longu Ram of *murabba* 357/44 in *chak* 13K was tied to a tree and tortured by some local hoodlums. He was finally murdered. The R & R department in Himachal lodged a complaint urging the Rajasthan authorities to take speedy action. But nothing has been done to date (Note on Resettlement and Rehabilitation of Pong Dam Oustees in the Rajasthan Canal Project Area, undated).

Land grabbing too is a severe problem. According to one report (Note on Resettlement and Rehabilitation of Pong Dam Oustees in the Rajasthan Canal Project Area, undated), about 200 *murabbas* belonging to Pong oustees were illegally occupied by armed gangs in October 1983. Although the area was later rid of the culprits, no action was taken against them.

When our team visited the area, the grave law and order situation as stated in the government reports (dated 1985–89) continued unabated. We met Shanti Devi, a widow who lived with her two sons and a daughter, on *murabba* 87/377 of *chak* 1 FDM. Her son, Inder Pal, had taken a loan of Rs 11,000 from Makhan Singh, a local resident, for a marriage in Kangra. Being illiterate, he had not known that he had put his thumb impression on a receipt which indicated the sale of his land for an amount of Rs 42,000. He stayed back to look after his land while the rest of his family went to Kangra for the wedding. On their return, they found Inder Pal missing from the *murabba* and Makhan Singh cultivating their land. Inder Pal has not been heard of since. Shanti Devi told us, 'Makhan Singh threatened us, warning us not to lodge a complaint. Now, we have become wage labourers on our own field. I have lost my son as well as my land.'

To quote a government report (Note on Resettlement and Rebahilitation of Pong Dam Oustees in Rajasthan Canal Project Area, 1987), 'Land-grabbers miss no opportunity to criminally trespass on the oustees' allotted lands. They are always on the look out to terrorise and harass the oustees to compel them to leave their allotted lands. They also connive with the local law-enforcing agencies.'

Mr Randhawa narrated one such case to our team. Hukum Chand Kotiya's father was allotted *murabba* 119/25 in 14P colony. Following his father's death, Hukum Chand had to get the *murabba* transferred in his name. He had to leave his land unattended for official work on 19 December 1984. On his return, he found that

Gurdeep Singh, a non-oustee, had cultivated 10 *bighas* of his land. When questioned, Gurdeep Singh told him that he had done so at the instance of the local *patwari*, Kishan Lal. The Hukum Chand then confronted the *patwari* who told him, 'This *murabba* is now in my possession, I will not let it go at any cost. If you wish, I can pay a sum of 15,000. If you try to intervene in any way, I will kill you.' (Taken from a letter written on 29 March 1986 by the *patwari* to Hukum Chand who sent a copy each to the Additional Colonisation Commissioner and Mi Randhawa.) Many other oustees had similar complaints against Kishan Lal, the *patwari*. He had taken illegal possession of *murabbas* belonging to Chuni Lal, Barfi Devi, Kartar Singh, Pyar Singh and Fakir Chand. But no action had been initiated against him.

All of them had approached Mr Randhawa who had written to the offices concerned in Rajasthan but there was no response. He then approached a sympathetic MLA from Himachal who took up the matter with the centre. It was only after the centre's intervention that the Rajasthan government was compelled to suspend the *patwari* towards the end of 1986.

The law and order situation was no better along the Indo-Pak border. There, too, the oustees were forcibly made to forego their lands. Jaisi Ram Khatta, as mentioned earlier, is now resettled in Bilaspur village, HP. He was allotted *murabba* 58/60 in *chak* 2P under phase II. But he found Dewan Singh, a non-oustee, cultivating his land. He told Dewan Singh of his allotment and asked him to vacate the land. In return; he was threatened. He told us, 'I was asked to leave the area. But when I did not do so, I was attacked by a group of armed men. I was lucky enough to save my life as I managed to escape. Nobody came to my help because everybody lives in constant fear of these people.'

Most of the plots restored to the oustees after cancellation were often found to be encroached upon by non-oustees and anti-social elements. These encroachers, in many cases, were able to obtain stay orders from the Court as soon as they realised that land had been allotted to an oustee. Mathura Devi, who was allotted land in 1976, was not allowed to deposit her instalment as the land was under a stay order. She said bitterly, 'In this place, we have to undergo punishment whenever the government people are at fault. Why did they not make enquiries before allotting me the disputed land? With the land, my source of livelihood has gone. But what troubles me even more is that I am not able to educate my children. There is no future for them.' According to one report (On-the-Spot Study, dated 1989), 81 cases of allotments on plots which were under a stay order were pending before the Additional Commissioner.

In addition to these problems, some powerful people were indulging in forgery of land documents. Our team was told by the HP officials at the Simla (R & R) office that non-oustees were forging land documents of the oustees' allotted lands. So far, 1,500 cases of forged documents had been reported. The officials felt that stringent action should be taken to put a stop to this practice.

The overall apathetic attitude of the local law enforcing authorities had encouraged anti-social elements. So much so that when the late J.C. Thapar (Deputy Collector of R & R, Talwara) visited colony 22 MD in 1985, he found the area cordoned off by about 25 armed men. He also came across another group of 30 armed men who were forcibly cutting the crops from 34 *murabbas*. He immediately reported the matter to the DIG, Bikaner, who sent an inspector to take charge of the situation. The inspector merely expressed his helplessness in the face of so many armed men.

In 1986, on Mr Thapar's next visit to Rajasthan, he was *gheraoed* by the local goons and was told 'not to come to Rajasthan again if he valued his life' (Note on Ressettlement and Rehabilitation of Pong Dam Oustees in Rajasthan Canal Command Area, by Shri J.C. Thapar, undated).

The majority of allotments in Anupgarh, Charanwala, as well as in other areas, were situated on the Indo-Pak border. Under the existing scenario, most oustees faced problems in retaining their lands due to cancellations, encroachments, law and order, etc. But the oustees in the vicinity of the Indo-Pak border had additional problems concerning their day to day living.

The oustees informed the team that their fields were situated so close to the border that 'many times, the front tip of our plough goes into the Pakistani territory.' They went on to add, 'We are living under the constant threat of being caught unawares in the crossfire between the two sides.'

Being close to the border, the mobility of the oustees was considerably restricted. Even during the day, their movements were closely monitored and they were required to get daily passes issued up to 5 p m from the BSF *chowkies*. At night, they could not move out of their houses unless special permission had been taken, which they could do only up to 5 p m. The oustees informed us that it was next to impossible to move out 'even if somebody needed help, particularly in cases of illness.'

This also prohibited them from working on their fields at night. To irrigate the fields, water was channelised to different areas in turn, either during the day or at night. Those whose turn to irrigate came at night were unable to do so as they were not permitted to venture out of their houses. This naturally affected the produce.

Not only was their everyday life bound by restrictions, but the smuggling activities across the border made the lives of the oustees even more difficult. On the one hand, the smugglers warned the oustees against giving any information to the authorities; on the other, the security forces conducted searches in their homes, sometimes during the day but mostly at night. Kishori Lal told us, 'An oustee was taken away at night by the police because they claimed that he was harbouring smugglers. We are falsely accused while the real culprits go scot free.' He added that this was a regular occurrence.

Undeniably, the general law and order situation and the overall unfavourable living conditions in Rajasthan were not conducive to the oustees to settling there.

Allotted Land Acquired Again

When the land was allotted, the authorities overlooked the fact that land would be required for developmental activities like *khalas*, *roads*, etc., which were to be a part of the irrigation network. As a matter of fact, this work, or at least the demarcations for the same, should have been completed before the allotments were made. However, the project authorities characteristically started this work long after the oustees took possession of their lands. Consequently, many oustees found that parts of their lands were being acquired. Many lost large portions of the land. Uttam Chand showed us his *murabba* where *khalas* had been constructed. He said, 'I have lost 5 *bighas* of my land. I approached the concerned officials several times with my problem. But the officials replied that since I did not have the title deed for the land, I was not entitled to any compensation.' In this case, although he had already paid the total cost of his land, he was yet to be handed the title papers which is a problem confronting a large number of other oustees as well. Whether or not it is justifiable, it appears that only a title holder was entitled to a hearing. But the majority of oustees were still in the process of paying the instalments, having invested large amounts of money towards the cost and development of their lands. For all practical purposes, both the title holders and others were meted out the same treatment by the government. Yet, one cannot but ask why the latter were not entitled to even a hearing. Thus, Uttam Chand's, like that of many others, is a no-win situation.

The oustees who had lost their lands owing to such developmental work demanded that either the government allot the amount of land lost or deduct the cost of the acquired piece of land from the net cost. The Rajasthan government, however, does not seem to think this fair and the problem remains unsolved.

On the border areas, the oustees' lands were also being acquired to fence the area for security reasons. According to one report (On-the-Spot Study, dated 1989), land up to almost 500 metres was being acquired along the border. As a result, many oustees had lost a substantial portion of their lands.

In some cases, lands measuring as much as half the size of the *murabba* had been acquired, for which the oustees had not received any compensation. They informed us that they had been instructed by the Rajasthan authorities to appeal to the BSF to deal with the matter. When the oustees did so, the BSF declined to compensate them in any manner stating that land was being acquired for a national cause.

In 1988, the Rajasthan government issued a notification declaring that all oustees residing along the border were encroachers and their *murabbas* would be cancelled (Himachal R & R department, Simla). This caused a lot of resentment amongst the oustees and they asked the Himachal government to intervene. Although the talks are still underway, the matter is yet to be resolved and the dispute continues.

Civic Amenities

HOUSING

As understood by the Rajasthan government, allotment of land to oustees was the only criterion for rehabilitation. None of the available documents on policy for resettlement and rehabilitation had referred to the issue of civic amenities. The Colonisation Rules of 1972 only mentioned that mud houses would be provided to the oustees, for which they would be required to pay. The amount of payment later fixed was Rs 1,500.

During our visit to the rehabilitation sites, we found that many of the houses were on the verge of collapse. According to the On-the-Spot Study (dated 1989) and the information from the Additional Commissioner, Rajasthan, out of a total of 4,173 houses constructed for the oustees, only 1,541 houses had remained intact. To add to the problems, of these 1,541 houses, as many as 1,287 houses were under the illegal possession of non-oustees.

The oustees informed us that their allotted houses were situated very far from their fields. 'This makes it difficult for us to till as well as guard our fields. We have to live in constant fear of losing our lands due to encroachment.'

Explaining their difficulties, the oustees said that every *chak abadi* was divided into two parts. One part had agricultural lands and the other was for houses. The distance between the house plots and lands even within the *chak* was at times 5 to 8 kilometres.

Many oustees were allotted houses and lands in two different *chaks*. In such cases, the distance was even greater and they had to travel approximately 15 to 20 km. Our team met a few families in 16P who were allotted houses in 19P, at a distance of 16 to 18 km from their agricultural plots. 'It is impossible to cover this distance twice a day,' they said.

This posed a serious problem for the oustees. According to the 1972 Rules, the oustees had to be present on their fields at the time of *girdawari* (field inspection) by the *patwari*, failing which the allotment was to be cancelled. Their absence from the fields at the time of *girdawari* was, in fact, one of the reasons why several allotments were cancelled under the first phase of resettlement. This problem was discussed at the ministerial meeting and the rule was amended in 1982. Now, the oustees could construct their own houses on their agricultural plots. This undoubtedly made it easier for them to protect their lands from encroachment and cancellation but they lost out on a part of their agricultural land which they used for the houses. They told us, 'We now do not have to walk long distances but we have lost out on a part of our lands and money in the bargain. We had to pay Rs 1,500 for the houses allotted to us, which we have not got back. Now, we have to spend on constructing new houses.'

One of the major factors due to which the oustees were unable to settle in Rajasthan was that civic amenities such as drinking water, educational and medical facilities, and electricity were not provided at the *chaks*. The Rules, on the other hand, made it imperative for the oustees to stay in *chak abadis*. During the cancellations, the authorities never considered the factors which compelled the oustees to live outside the *chak abadis*. For them, mere adherence to the Rules was what mattered most.

DRINKING WATER

The oustees resettled in the first phase received drinking water facilities only in 1975–76 and those resettled under the second phase, in 1986. Diggies (cemented tanks) were meant to be provided as a source of drinking water, but only a few colonies were given this facility. Mr Randhawa, who was allotted land in 20P of Anupgarh, said, 'The oustees of the first phase have been the worst off. Those who were resettled sometime from 1965–66 onwards, (i.e. during phase I), had to do without water for almost a decade. Later, wherever diggies were provided, the source of water was from *khalas* only.'

The Rajasthan authorities had prepared a plan to filter water from *khalas* or minor canals through diggies to be channelised into wells. But obviously this plan remained on paper alone (On-the-Spot Evaluation Study, dated 1989).

Randhawa added, 'Till 1976, there were no diggies in my colony and we had to use running water from the same *khala* for both drinking and washing purposes. This water was used even to feed our cattle. This was naturally unfit for drinking.'

As matters stood in 1989, even colonies with a large concentration of oustees were not equipped with any drinking water facility. Approximately 400 families settled in 22A colony of Anupgarh, were not provided with a single diggy (On-the-Spot Evaluation Study, dated 1989). Similarly, during our visit to the offices of the Himachal government, we were informed that the situation in this regard was so pathetic that as many as 385 families in Suratgarh were forced to do without any drinking water facilities. This study also mentioned that since resettlement the authorities had still not woken up to the gravity of the existing situation. To date, the oustees are managing by diverting water from *khalas* or minor canals into small *kuccha* pits or tanks.

SCHOOLS

There were only four primary schools for 41 colonies in four *tehsils*. There were even fewer middle and high schools. For instance, in Anupgarh *tehsil*, there was only one middle school at Gharsana for all the surrounding colonies. Those who wished to study up to high school had to travel to Anupgarh town, covering a distance of 15 to 20 km. That posed a difficulty since there were no link roads in the *chaks* and as such no transport was available. Naturally, it was difficult for the oustees to send their children to schools at such a distance. They told us that although private schools had come up in some areas, they were expensive and most could not afford to send their children there. The primary school in 6P colony had 150 students but only two teachers. Our team visited this school and found the students playing, with no teacher in attendance. We spoke to a student, Lal Chand, who said, 'Our teacher has gone to Anupgarh on some personal matter. Therefore, we have been given a holiday.'

If the oustees wanted to apply for jobs or seek admission for their children for higher studies, they were required to produce domicile certificates. These certificates were to have been issued to oustees who had settled in Rajasthan. But the government had not issued any such certificates and the children were being sent out of the state to study. 'On the one hand', said the oustees, 'the government is making new schemes to eradicate illiteracy; on the other, our children are unable to study as there are no schools. All that our children are learning to do is graze cattle.'

MEDICAL FACILITIES

There are only eight primary health centres for 41 colonies. In 6P colony, a dispensary had been constructed by 1970. But till 1987, no doctor or compounder had arrived to take charge. The local *chowkidar* was using the building as his residence. The nearest medical care centres for 6P colony were at Gharsana and Anupgarh and none of them were connected by bus. Therefore, the oustees had to hire jeeps during emergencies; a one-way trip cost them Rs 50!

The lack of any government medical facilities, needless to say, had encouraged the mushrooming of a corps of quacks who were making good money exploiting the people.

OTHER FACILITIES

Only a few colonies had been electrified. Post-offices were situated only at the *tehsil* or district level towns, and the oustees made weekly trips to collect their mail. For example, letters for oustees of Anupgarh and Gharsana *tehsils* had to be collected from Sohan Singh in Anupgarh.

The oustees complained that unlike the local people, they were not being covered by the various rural development schemes like IRDP, RLEGP and Rozgar Yojana. Since they were not given domicile certificates, the facility for loans to develop their lands was also not extended to them as they were not considered citizens of the state. A high-level officer of the Rajasthan government held discussions with a delegation of Himachal officials concerning the problems of the oustees. During the course of this meeting, he categorically told the HP team that the oustees could not be given facilities similar to those enjoyed by the local people.

Later, when a group of oustees met some of the officials concerned with regard to this, they were told to take their problems to 'their own government'. They told us, 'We cannot be treated like second rate citizens if the Rajasthan government wants us to settle here. How can they expect us to keep running back to the Himachal government for every little problem? But that is what we have been doing because the Rajasthan government does not listen to us.'

In the report, Note on Resettlement and Rehabilitation of Pong Dam Oustees in Rajasthan Canal Area, undated, the Himachal officials had stated that mere allotment of land cannot be considered rehabilitation of oustees. Until all the benefits provided to other people in Rajasthan are extended to them, they would continue to feel alienated. The Rajasthan authorities obviously think differently.

Conclusion

Nineteen years had passed since the protest at the Pong dam site in 1970. It was now 1989. Standing next to the canal at Anupgarh colony in Rajasthan, Kishori Lal made a poignant comment: 'The water you see in the canal is in reality blood, ours and our children's.' Melodramatic though it sounds, it stands in stark contrast to the picture portrayed by the project authorities, both before and after the project became a reality. Visits to various rehabilitation sites revealed that the prevailing mood among the oustees was one of helpless despondency, while the future seemed even more bleak. The question is: what went wrong and where?

With the wisdom of hindsight, it is now obvious that most of the problems of the oustees could have been avoided. To begin with, the project authorities did not prepare a time-bound programme for rehabilitation which should have been ready well in advance of the actual displacement. Not only was this not done, even the Colonisation Rules for allotment of land were framed as late as 1972, after 572 families had already been displaced since 1965.

Ostensibly, the Pong oustees were entitled to a share in the benefits from the project as they were, according to the policy, to be given land in the command area of the dam, and they should have had no cause for complaint. Only, the project authorities overlooked certain basic factors and the consequences are there for all to see. They failed to realise that:

a The command zone fell in an area which was a virtual desert;
b The land for allotment was completely uncultured and undeveloped and as such needed heavy investment in terms of labour and cash;
c No irrigation facility was available at the time of allotment, or even years after at many sites; and
d The Rules governing the allotment of land and its cultivation within an impossibly short span of time negated the very purpose of allotment.

Inevitably, the allotted plot of land proved to be a liability instead of a viable economic asset. In the final analysis, then, despite being entitled to land in the command area, the oustees, for all practical purposes, remained bereft of this benefit.

It is a reflection of the government's attitude that the manner in which they conducted the process of resettlement was extremely ill-planned and unsystematic to say the least. For instance, a large number of oustees would have been spared the anguish of losing their lands due to cancellations, and the problem of encroachments could have been checked to some extent, if the authorities had *a* identified pockets where irrigation facilities had been made available and made allotments accordingly; and *b* equipped the resettlement sites with at least the basic civic amenities so as to make them habitable. Again, their resettlement in large blocks, ensuring that they were not outnumbered by non-oustees, would have acted as a deterrent against encroachment.

The record of the Rajasthan authorities over the last 25 years undoubtedly indicates that they flouted many of the clauses under the Rules, both in word and spirit. The most serious among them related to the stipulation of reserving an area of 2.25 lakh acres exclusively for resettlement purposes before actual displacement took place. Not only did the authorities not reserve this entire chunk, but they did not even identify the same. Furthermore, no rehabilitation sites were formed separately for the displaced families. They were made to live with the local people. However, the authorities made no effort to prepare either the host population or the oustees for a new life. A large number of oustees had to pay for this lapse, in a number of ways, and many with their lives.

But that was not all. The local people were allotted or auctioned land out of the reserved area. Naturally, land for the oustees fell short and they were given land outside the command and reserved area, many of them in the border areas. Cancellations followed, reapplications were made and the cycle continues. How and when it will end is a question that even the Rajasthan authorities find themselves unable to answer!

The situation was summed up by Mr Randhawa, thus: 'What have we got? Children of many oustee families have only learnt to graze cattle. The later generations will be even worse off. Is this development? There is so much poverty in India and the government says they will remove it. But they are doing the opposite. Look at us. Mere lip service to the sacrifice we made for the country will not get us our daily bread. If the government goes on building dams like this, then the poor and backward people will die.'

6

Baliraja: A People's Alternative

ENAKSHI GANGULY THUKRAL •
MACHHINDRA D. SAKATE

The story of the Baliraja dam is important in more ways than one. It is a practical solution to a situation of drought, with the use of local resources. It does not result in any displacement and, most important, it is a result of the people's own initiative. It is *their* solution to *their* problem.

The farmers of Balwadi and Tendulwadi villages of Khanapur *taluka* in Sangli district of Maharashtra once grew sugar-cane and other water-intensive crops in plenty, so much so that they used to dump the excess at the *taluka* office or even burn it as they did in 1981 (Vijaypurkar 1987). Problems began when droughts became frequent and the Yerala river around which their lives revolved suddenly began to dry up. It is at this juncture that our story of the Baliraja Smriti dam begins.

The Genesis

The river Yerala is a tributary of the Krishna flowing through the Satara and Sangli districts of Maharashtra. Till recently it was a

Note: This paper is based on a study by Machhindra D. Sakate. The fieldwork was done entirely by Sakate, and the study was commissioned by MARG in 1987. We are grateful to Mr Rajendra Patil for his guidance to Sakate during the study.

perennial river but the drought of 1972 changed everything. The river started drying up and the once plentiful flow of water ceased. Except for about 15 days during the peak monsoons, the river now remained dry the rest of the year.

The dry sand-bed of the river caught the attention of contractors who began large-scale and reckless mining of sand from the river-bed without concern for the impact this might have on ground water retention. As a result, all the rain water during the monsoons started to flow directly into the Krishna, taking with it the precious top-soil as there were no trees or forests left in the catchment area of the river to bind it.

With the river drying up, the depleted sand-bed in the river basin was unable to permit percolation of water. This, coupled with the deforestation in the catchment areas, resulted in a fall of the water-table. Wells started drying up. Problems of drinking water, especially in the villages along the banks of the river, assumed serious proportions.

The problem of drought and its concomitant scarcity, and the inability of the authorities concerned to deal with the situation, forced the people to take matters into their own hands. The villagers of Balwadi and Tendulwadi decided it was time to find a practical solution to their problems and implement it unitedly.

They decided to construct a dam—4.5 metres high and 120 metres long—across the Yerala to enable protective irrigation and help solve the drinking water problem. Thus, the idea of the 'Baliraja Smriti' dams was born.

Khanapur *Taluka*

With a total area of 13,268 sq km, Khanapur *taluka* of Sangli district has a population of 2,18,000 (1981 census figures), of whom 1,11,000 are females. It has a rural population of 1,94,000.

The average rainfall, according to the irrigation department, is 23 inches, but the Balwadi (Bhalvani) dam office (which is now closed) records an average rainfall of 12 inches. A total area of 11,018 sq km is under cultivation.

The Nandini, Agarni and Yerala are the three major rivers flowing through this *taluka*. Of the three, the Yerala is the largest and, as mentioned earlier, was, till the 1970s, a perennial river.

The frequency and intensity of droughts seem to have reached serious proportions only in the latter part of the 20th century. Continuous dry spells combined with deforestation, use of scarce water for water-intensive crops like sugar-cane and large-scale excavation of sand from the river-bed has aggravated the situation. The conditions of drought in the area forced the people to migrate in search of alternative sources of livelihood. Many went to work at textile mills in Bombay.

In 1973 the Government of Maharashtra appointed the Sukhathankar Committee to study the drought-prone areas, classify them and suggest remedies. The Committee declared 89 *talukas* of 14 districts as drought-prone. Of these, six *talukas* were located in the Krishna basin, of which four belonged to Sangli district of the state. Khanapur *taluka* was one of the four drought-prone *talukas* of Sangli district.

The Committee, however, did not look deeper into the causes of drought in the area, nor did it take a firm stand on its eradication. It concerned itself mainly with interim drought relief programmes.

Mukti Sangharsha Chalval

The long strike by the cotton mill workers of Bombay saw the in-migration of these workers to their villages. The striking mill workers and the drought affected masses assembled together, thought together and, as a result, the Mukti Sangharsha Chalval (Struggle for Liberation Movement) was born. It was a broad platform of left-wing activists and included active participants and leaders such as Bhai Sampatrao Pawar, Dr Bharat Patankar, Dr Gail Omvedt, Mani and Joy, to name a few.

The struggle was intensified for the fulfilment of their demands which included: work under the Employment Guarantee Schemes (EGS) be made available, an end be put to the rampant corruption of officials in the EGS, and provision for drinking water and other facilities like creches be made.

Agitations and strikes were organised, cases of corruption were exposed. A mass education movement to remove ignorance and r superstitious beliefs amongst various communities was organised. The Phule-Ambedkar Thoughts Movement was organised for the effective inculcation of feelings of brotherhood and unity. Efforts were also made to organise movements around the problems of the nomadic and *vimukta* people.

During the course of these agitations, the Chalval realised that the most serious problem in the area at the time was that of recurring droughts. A special plan of action was urgently required to fight it and an effort was made to organise the agitation around the on-going drought conditions.

As a first step, a scientific study of all the waterways, wells and irrigation facilities was undertaken by the Chalval. It was found that Khanapur *taluka* had no major irrigation project. It had one medium project, the Yeralwadi Medium Irrigation Project. This was supposed to provide 2.03 million cusecs of water to only 290 hectares of land. According to the irrigation department there were 10 minor irrigation projects in Khanapur *taluka*.

One of the minor dams, the Balwadi dam, which is upstream of the site for the Baliraja dam on the river Yerala, was built in the late 1950s but has not lived up to its expectations. The local people remember a season when it did not irrigate even 20 hectares of the targeted 460 hectares of the command area, even though it has a 26 km long canal. The canal had been deepened a number of times under the EGS but the dam continued to get silted.

Besides these projects, there were 73 percolation tanks in the *taluka*. All these projects and tanks together, according to government estimates, were irrigating only 8.4 per cent of the total cultivable land. A survey conducted by the Mukti Sangharsha Chalval, however, revealed that less than 2 per cent of the total cultivable land was actually being irrigated.

During the course of their survey the following facts were brought to light:

1. The government machinery had not scientifically studied the root cause of the recurrence of drought in that particular area.
2. Until the basic and fundamental cause of drought was established the problem could not be tackled.
3. There was no planning on how to deal with the situation at the governmental level.
4. Huge sums of money were being spent under the Employment Guarantee Scheme on unproductive work which was not even remotely related to dealing with the situation of drought.

5. The various government departments—irrigation, soil conservation, social forestry—worked as independent units with
no coordination between them. As a result, the impact of
governmental programmmes was piecemeal and *ad hoc.*

In 1984 the Chalval organised a 10 day Vigyan Yatra or Science
Fair in 11 villages of Khanapur-Vita *taluka* on the specific problems
faced due to droughts. It also focused on the more general problems
related to agriculture in the area. Its objectives were to educate
the people, to provide them with a scientific outlook, and to instil
in them the belief that their problems could be solved by proper
planning and scientific methods.

Awakened by such education and convinced about the possibility
of finding effective solutions, the people began agitations, raising
slogans like 'we will not break stones, we will not construct roads,
we will not rest till the drought is eradicated'.[1] Piecemeal measures
like relief works would no more be accepted, they said. They laid
emphasis on the creation of productive assets that would reduce
their hardship and ensure future returns from the land. As part of
their agitation they highlighted the findings of the survey.

The people believed that the cause of repeated droughts in the
area was not natural but man-made, a product of bad planning.
They were of the firm opinion that both drought relief and eradication could be achieved though a single programme of action. Thus,
the Dushkal Nirmulan Parishad (Council for Drought Eradication)
was convened on 27 October 1985.

Excavation of Sand

The Yerala river dried up revealing a dry sand-bed which made
excellent construction material. This immediately attracted the
attention of contractors.

Large-scale excavation of sand began. The calculation was simple.
To obtain a permit to lift 100 brass (100 cft) of sand, Rs 1,000 was
required to be paid as royalty to the government and the average
selling rate varied from Rs 60 to 70 per brass (1 cft). The quarrying
took place either through time-bound permits or through auctions.

---

[1] Under the EGS's Food for Work programme, people were employed to break
and remake roads.

The motive of both the private contractors and the government was profit-making. They employed the local villagers for labour and since the people were in dire need, the immediate gains from sand excavation offered them relief. They earned Rs 60 to 80 per day working as labourers, loading sand on to the trucks.

Therefore no effort was made to limit the volume of sand lifted or to assess the ecological consequences of such large-scale quarrying. As drought conditions intensified, so did the sand transport business.

As the geological structure of the Deccan basalt rocks in this area does not permit percolation of water, the layers of sand in the river-bed helped retain water from where it percolated to the numerous jack wells in the river-bed as well as wells on the banks. In the days when the river was perennial, the sand was lifted only in summer when the river dried up. The sand bed was replenished by nature's own mechanism.

Disproportionate exploitation of water for water-intensive crops and excessive mining of sand disturbed this equilibrium. The silt and clay that was left behind formed a hard impervious surface, blocking the percolation of water.. This resulted in acute water scarcity. Wells began drying up. The survey carried out by the Mukti Sangharsh Chalval in 1983 showed that by December 1980, 100 of the 122 jack wells in the river-bed had dried up (Rao 1989: 2).

As the movement grew, so did awareness of the ecological consequences of such indiscriminate mining of sand. The villagers decided that the only way to counter such large-scale depletion of sand, restore the ecological balance and also solve their water problems, would be to construct a dam across the Yerala that would ensure storage of water in the river-bed.

After seeking technical advice from well-wishers, they found such a possibility could be given concrete shape. Taking inspiration from the contractors who were making profits by selling sand, the villagers of Balwadi and Tendulwadi, on opposite banks of the Yerala, decided to raise the necessary funds for the project by excavating and selling sand on a limited scale. In this way they would be able to raise the funds without seeking any financial aid from the government. At the same time, the money derived from the sale of sand from the river-bed would be used to return wealth to the Yerala in the form of water. Thus, the idea of the Baliraja

Smriti dam, named after the famous mythological peasant king known for his compassion, justice and equitable treatment of all, took concrete shape.

Actual Progress

A proposal to build a dam across the Yerala was submitted to the Collector of Sangli on 26 October 1986. The proposal laid out that indiscriminate mining of sand from the Yerala bed should be stopped. It suggested instead that permits for the sale of a specified amount of sand at reasonable rates be issued to the people. With the proceeds from these sales and with *shramadana* (voluntary labour), the people would construct a dam across the river.

Some officials, however, insisted on their purchasing permits on the basis of auction sales. This stricture was finally withdrawn due to the persistent efforts of the Chalval.

The excavation for the foundation of the dam began on 23 November 1986 at the hands of Shri Chandrakant Ghorpade former editor of the Pune-based newspaper *Kesari*. The excavation was undertaken through *shramadana* by the students of four colleges from Vita, Khadepur, Tasgaon and Ramanand Nagar which are affiliated to the Shivaji University, Kolhapur, and by the villagers of Balwadi and Tendulwadi.

The dam—120 metres long and 4.5 metres high—with a storage capacity of 20 million cft of water was designed by K.R. Datye, a progressive consulting engineer from Bombay. He prepared the necessary plans and estimates free of cost, which, according to him, was 'technical *shramadana*'.

The foundation stone of the Baliraja dam was formally laid on 25 January 1987 by Smt Laxmibai Naikwadi, wife of late Shri Naganath Naikwadi, a close associate of Nana Patil.

Problems Begin

The construction of the dam had reached a height of one foot above the level of the river-bed when the scenario changed suddenly. The construction of the dam was declared illegal by the government and the District Collector ordered the suspension of construction work. However, no written official order was issued by him. Since the Yerala was a 'denotified' river, all that was required was a 'no objection certificate' from Bombay.

After days of intense struggle marked by demonstrations and *dharnas*, the Collector decided to send the proposal for clearance to the *mantralaya* (the state secretariat).

The Government of Maharashtra agreed to hold discussions with the members of the Chalval. These discussions and meetings began on 25 June 1987.

In the meantime, permits for the sale of sand continued to be issued to private contractors though contracts to the Chalval were firmly refused.

Getting the official sanction took well over a year. 'What upset the authorities was that they found themselves superfluous to the entire process . . . . The Collector of Sangli district commented that, "the Government never reversed its stance. It was slow to respond initially and without pressure from the villagers, it may have never moved on its own. But there was no opposition to the dam itself" . . .' (Kurien 1989).

On 24 February 1989 the government finally revoked the stay and issued official permission for them to continue construction. The people celebrated the day as 'Victory Day'. Work at the site was resumed.

As work progressed, new problems began to emerge. For specialised and technical aspects of dam construction, it was necessary to use skilled labour which required money. Cement and other raw materials too required large sums of money. Permits for the mining and sale of only 1,900 brass of sand had been issued to the Chalval. Only Rs 85,000 could be collected from sand sales, of which Rs 20,000 had to be paid to the Government as royalty. Work therefore began with a mere Rs 65,000 while the government refused to issue fresh permits. The construction was thus once again held up, this time due to financial constraints. A minimum of Rs 1.5 to 2 lakhs was the immediate requirement.

To overcome this financial crisis, the possibilities of raising interest-free loans were explored. Appeals were made to individual well-wishers and money was borrowed from various sections of society and organisations in Bombay and Pune. The amount borrowed was to be refunded after the completion of the dam. With the money raised a Drought Eradication Fund was set up to tide over this difficulty.

But the people were not to be deterred by all these problems. 'This is our dam. Let anyone oppose it. We will not rest till it is completed. We will sacrifice our blood for the completion of this dam and it will be completed,' they said with conviction.

Baliraja—A New Path

An analysis of the plans prepared by K.R. Datye revealed a number of interesting facts. Here was a project that was to be constructed by the people on an incredibly low budget and without the problem of displacement due to submergence. The salient features of the Baliraja dam project are:

1. Total length of dam : 120 metres
2. Height of dam : 4.5 metres
3. Live storage : 20.5 million cft
4. Irrigation potential : 380 hectares
5. Estimated increase in production : 2.8 tonnes/hectares

The dam was to be built in two phases. In the first phase the dam was to be constructed up to a height of 2.5 metres with conventional masonry work. The second phase was to include the installation of a pressure gate (falling shutters) 2 metres high, for which Mr. Datye and his team worked on a low-cost design. This reduction in cost was to be achieved by using a combination of small dimension timber and ferro-cement instead of the conventional steel plates.

The Balwadi *bhandara* (Balwadi dam which has been silted up) was located one km upstream of the Baliraja dam site. This Balwadi *bhandara* was to arrest a large amount of the silt flow, especially the coarse sand. The existence of this *bhandara* upstream and the construction of four conventional screen gates, planned by Mr. Datye, was to result in a very low rate of siltation.

The project was to be completed at a cost of approximately Rs 3,09,000, but would have cost much less had the government been more sympathetic.

In spite of these financial constraints, the people's determination never waned. People from various walks of life came forward to help and extend their cooperation to this novel venture. Sixteen lawyers from the Sangli District Bar Association offered their *shramadana* for construction work. The entire staff of the Karamvir Bhaurao Patil Vidyalaya, Islampur, expressed a similar desire. One hundred home guards from Sangli district offered *shramadana* for 10 days. Besides, there was the constant support of students and members of the Shivaji University. This truly was 'Victory of the People'.

The signficance of the dam lies not so much in itself as in the concepts underlying it: that water belongs to every member of society irrespective of caste, sex or creed, and that a viable efficient system is possible only if the community is committed to it.

According to Dr Bharat Patankar of the Mukti Sangharsh Chalval, the dam has to be seen in the context of the drought situation in Maharashtra and not as an alternative in itself.

Equal Distribution of Water

The people decided that the water was to be shared equitably for crops that were not water-intensive. All villagers were part of the 'water users' cooperative' and water was to be distributed according to the following rules:

1. Every member would be entitled to a share of the water irrespective of his/her sex or caste. Each family would get a share according to family size and not according to the size of the landholding. A maximum of five members per family would be entitled to shares.
2. Even the landless (there were only three landless families in Balwadi and Tendulwadi) would be entitled to shares which they could either sell or use by taking on lease someone's land on a sharecropping basis.
3. Each share would cost Rs 10 or one days's *shramadana* on the dam site.
4. Water was to be made available in fortnightly stretches from 1 June to 15 January for protective irrigation of non-water-intensive crops like jowar, millet and ground-nut. From 15 January each year, water would be reserved for drinking purposes.

5. Drinking water equivalent to the requirement of 5,000 persons would be kept as 'reserved storage' and a certain amount would be used for biomass production and the development of nurseries. It was the aim of the cooperative to develop 0.02 hectares of silvi-horticultural land per adult over the next five years.

6. The cropping pattern of the area under command was to be worked out in consultation with all the members in conformity with the above principles before the rabi and kharif seasons and it would be obligatory for the members to conform to it in order to receive water.

Each member had to take a pledge to abide by these rules. According to the pledge:

> Everybody, irrespective of whether he/she is rich or poor, has equal right over the water given by nature and stored by the efforts of common labour in which he/she has actively participated. Nobody should have special benefits in any way, is my firm belief and conviction. For such a distribution system based on the principle of equality, a crop pattern aimed at high yield can be finalised in consultation with all. I abide by this principle.

To ensure the success of this distribution pattern, the Baliraja Memorial Dam Committee was established. Keeping in mind the needs of various sections of society, each section was represented in the 11-member Committee. Two women also found representation. They were authorised to issue water-share certificates. This pattern of distribution was welcomed by the women who for the first time were involved in the decision-making process. According to Dr Bharat Patankar, 'it was the active participation of women in this whole process that has ultimately resulted in their being able to get their rightful share of the water—something that would be traditionally opposed by the men.'

The Baliraja Water Development and Water Distribution Society is now a registered trust but it was to be given the status of a water user's cooperative which would see to the distribution of water, maintenance and other related aspects of the system.

The water distribution system and cropping pattern were supposed to be put to test in 40 hectares of land in Tendulwadi village in the kharif season of 1989. The first gate of the dam was inaugurated on 5 March 1989. The water distribution system has now enabled the landless women, Ranjana Aklushswali and Draupadi Vittalwadi, for instance, to share the benefits. 'The water can be sold to the landed peasants and it will help supplement my income,' said Ranjana, who had been deserted by her husband and left to fend for herself as well as six members of her family (Kurian 1989). Extensive agro-forestry in the catchment area is also being planned to restore ecological balance and reduce erosion.

It is not to say that small dams like the Baliraja are always the solution. The solutions have to be location- and situation-specific. What is important is that the solution must be based on people's needs and involve their participation. That is what makes the Baliraja Smriti Dam important. As Sampat Rao Pawar, a leading figure and the brain behind the dam says, 'this is the dam of the people, for and by the people. This is the beginning of a struggle . . . the government has no concrete plans of action for drought eradication, so the people will have to find their own solutions. Baliraja is the solution. It is not only a dam, it is a new direction.'

References

Kurian, Priya. 1989. *Times of India*. 13 March.
Rao, Nagamani. 1989. Baliraja Smriti Dam: The People's Dam. *Wastelands News*. August–October.
Vijaypurkar, Mahesh. 1987. For a People's Dam. *Frontline*. 31 October–13 November.

7

Rehabilitation Laws and Policies: A Critical Look

KALPANA VASWANI

Introduction

The decades since Independence have witnessed an accelerated pace of economic development in the country and there has been a tremendous spurt in the number of development projects taken up by the state. This has resulted in the compulsory acquisition of land from private citizens in order to subserve the 'common good'. As a consequence, thousands of people have been compelled to leave their homes and disrupt the way of life built up by their forefathers. In the circumstances, one would expect there to be at the national/state level a clearly defined policy with regard to the re-settlement and rehabilitation of such persons. But this is not the case.

Let us critically examine the laws which permit the acquisition of private land and the nature of recompense provided for such acquisition along with the existing policy guidelines on the subject at the national/state level.

The Land Acquisition Act, 1894

The principal law (central) which deals exclusively with the subject of acquisition of private land by the state is the Land Acquisition

Act of 1894 (henceforth referred to as the Act). This Act now applies to the whole of India except the state of Jammu and Kashmir which has its own enactment in this regard.

As this Act was enacted at a time when the role of the state in promoting public welfare and economic development was negligible, its provisions are obviously not in consonance with the social and economic realities of today. Since Independence, the role of the state in promoting economic development has expanded greatly. And, on the social front, it is no longer sufficient for the state to merely maintain law and order. The state is now expected to actively advance the welfare of its citizens. Consequently, both the central and the state governments have been making increasing use of the provisions of the Act to acquire land for such diverse public purposes as the setting up of thermal power stations, multi-purpose irrigation projects, planned development of a particular area, widening of public roads, military purposes, construction of post-offices, hospitals, reconstruction of damaged places of worship, etc. In many cases the extent of land acquired involves the displacement of an entire village or even a group of villages as, for example, in the case of large irrigation projects.

The gravest shortcoming of this Act is that it provides for the payment of cash compensation alone for land compulsorily acquired under its provisions and that too only to those who have a direct or indirect interest in the title to such land or the compensation payable for it (see definition of 'person interested' in Section 3 of the Act). The landless for instance, labourers in the agricultural and non-agricultural sectors, artisans and forest produce collectors, who form an integral part of the social and economic fabric of the village community and who will also be forced to start the struggle for life afresh, apparently do not need to be recompensed for the destruction of a way of life often built up over decades.

The Act neither contains any provision for allotting alternate land of a comparable quality to those whose land has been acquired, nor does it make it obligatory for the authority acquiring the land to assume the responsibility of resettling and rehabilitating those displaced by the acquisition. With the payment of cash compensation, the responsibility of the state ceases.

By virtue of an amendment introduced in the Act in 1984, the government (central as well as state) can now acquire land for the purpose of providing residential accommodation to those who have been affected or displaced by reason of the implementation of any scheme undertaken by the government, any local authority or a state owned or controlled corporation such as the Fertiliser Corporation of India or the National Thermal Power Corporation (see 3 (f) (v) of the Act). The fact that such a provision has been introduced indicates that the government is aware of the plight of those displaced on account of the acquisition of their land under the Act and has thought it necessary to arm itself with the power to acquire land for the resettlement of such persons. However, this is merely an enabling provision; it does not make it obligatory for the government to acquire alternate residential land for those who have lost their homes due to acquisition under the Act. Given that almost all available land is occupied, by exercising the power conferred by this provision the government will only be displacing another set of people who in turn will have to be resettled!

Experience has shown that payment of compensation in cash to the displaced is not an adequate solution to the problems faced by them. The bulk of those displaced by development projects are the poor, the illiterate and many of them tribals who are not capable of investing the compensation wisely. Once this money has been squandered they are left quite destitute. Other measures need to be adopted in order to effectively resettle and rehabilitate those whose land has been acquired under the Act.

Rights of a Displaced Person

Today, as matters stand, a person whose land is acquired under the provisions of the Act and who is consequently forced to uproot himself and put down roots in a new and often hostile environment has no legally enforceable right except the right to be compensated for the land that he lost, and that too at rates that are generally well below the prevailing market prices. The reason for this inequitable situation is that the Act provides for payment of compensation on the basis of the rates prevailing at the time the government issued notification under Section 4 of the Act announcing that it may consider acquiring the land described in such a notification. Under the existing provisions of the Act, as many as three years may elapse between the time that the notification under Section 4 is issued and the time the Collector makes his award adjudicating the compensation payable to the displaced. Even if the award is made, there is no guarantee that payment will be forthcoming as the Act prescribes no time frame within which the compensation must be paid once the award has been made. There is provision only for payment of interest in the event of delay in payment once the Collector takes possession of the land in question. Such a policy obviously works to the disadvantage of the displaced as the compensation they receive is generally inadequate and does not enable them to purchase alternate land of a comparable quality at the current spiralling prices.

The position of a displaced person who has no legal interest in the land acquired even though he may be dependent on it for his livelihood is even more pitiable for he does not even have the right to receive any compensation for the havoc wreaked by the acquisition.

In the circumstances, one is forced to ask: To what avail are the Constitutional guarantees of the right to settle anywhere in the country, the right to conserve one's culture, the right to follow an occupation of one's choice, the right to enjoy life and personal liberty? These are all fundamental rights that have been guaranteed by the Constitution, subject to the power of the state to impose reasonable restrictions on the exercise of those rights in the interests of the general public, public order decency, morality, integrity of the country, etc.

The last few years have witnessed the expansion of the scope of Article 21 which guarantees the right to life and personal liberty. The Supreme Court has in several cases held that the right to live is not merely confined to physical existence but includes within its ambit the right to live with human dignity and all that this entails: the bare necessities of life such as adequate nutrition, clothing, shelter and facilities for reading, writing and expressing oneself in diverse forms, moving freely and mixing and co-mingling with fellow human beings (*Francis Coralie* vs *Union Territory of Delhi*, AIR (1978 SC 597).

In a subsequent case the Supreme Court went further and held that the right to livelihood and the right to work are a part of the right to life (*Olga Tellis* vs *Bombay Municipal Corporation*, 1985, 3 SCC 545).

In a Calcutta case the ruling in the Olga Tellis case was used by the public interest petitioners to enforce their right to work and livelihood. The petitioners were a large number of hutment and : shanty dwellers residing along the canals, who were to be evicted by the Municipal Corporation of Calcutta so that proper flushing of all sewage and rain water was not hindered. These dwellers included refugees from East Pakistan and victims of communal riots. They argued that since they had no place to live, they had been forced to reside by the sides of canals and had been earning their livelihood through various avocations of life in and around the place where they lived in the city of Calcutta. If the Corporation was allowed to demolish their dwellings without assuring their rehabilitation, they would be deprived of their right to livelihood guaranteed to them under Article 21.

The Calcutta High Court agreed that in the *Olga Tellis* case the Supreme Court had interpreted Article 21 as including a right to livelihood but in that case too the pavement and slum dwellers were denied any right to use the pavement or any other public place which would cause annoyance or inconvenience to the general public. The High Court held that the petitioners had no fundamental right to use public properties and the Corporation was free to demolish their dwellings even though they were compelled to reside along the canals due to extreme poverty and helplessness. The Court agreed that on eviction they would be deprived of their means of livelihood, yet it refused to issue directions to the government to provide alternate sites for other rehabilitation (Matter No. 57, Block Bastuhara Committee, AIR, 1987, Cal 123).

It has been observed that the right to livelihood and the right to work remain very feeble and ineffective fundamental rights, incapable of being enforced by judicial action. 'It remains, therefore, unexplained what social purpose has been served by the Courts in unduly expanding and reconceptualising the right to life under Article 21 without carrying any burden to fulfil the enlarged (commitment' (Annual Survey of Indian Law 1987).

In view of the appalling prospect facing a person whose land is compulsorily acquired by the government, not only the right to life guaranteed by Article 21 of the Constitution but the various freedoms guaranteed by Article 19 too would seem to them to be nothing more than 'paper' rights. Restrictions on the rights guaranteed by the Constituion without adequate justification are *ultra vires*.

The reasonableness of such restrictions is a justiciable issue. But how many of those affected by the Act (keeping in mind the poverty and illiteracy of those generally displaced), have the resources to challenge such an infringement of their rights? And even if some do manage to file writ petitions in the Courts, in the absence of a clearly defined national rehabilitation policy applicable to all projects of a certain magnitude (in terms of the number of people displaced), what effective relief can the Court grant if it does come to the conclusion that the restrictions are indeed reasonable and in the interest of the general public?

This then brings us to the need for a comprehensive national policy/legislation on the subject of resettlement and rehabilitation of those displaced on account of the compulsory acquisition of their land by the state.

In 1985 the Committee on the Rehabilitation of Displaced Tribals due to Development Projects, Ministry of Home Affairs, Government of India, recommended that a national policy covering all categories of displaced persons, rather than tribals alone, should be evolved incorporating certain features. It suggested that the rehabilitation of displaced persons should form an integral part of all projects of a certain magnitude, whether such projects are being executed by the government or corporations in the joint, public or private sectors. It further advocated that once such a national policy was framed it should have legal authority and be binding on the government so that it could be effectively implemented.

Nearly five years have elapsed since these recommendations were put forward but no significant headway has been made towards the formulation of such a national policy. Nor has any national body been established to set the process in motion.

Laws/Policies of the State Governments

The grim reality with which we are faced today is that despite the fact that thousands of people have been uprooted from their homes as a result of the acquisition of their land for development projects, there is no law on the subject of their rehabilitation save in the states of Maharashtra and Madhya Pradesh. However, a fact that is little known is that even the Madhya Pradesh Pariyojana Ke

Karan Visthapit Vyakti (Punhsthapan) Adhiniyam, 1985 (the MP Act) and the Maharashtra Project Affected Persons Rehabilitation Act 1986 (the Maharashtra Act) are not automatically applicable to all projects in these states.

The MP Act has left it to the discretion of the state government to decide whether or not it is necessary to apply the provision of Act to a particular project. In effect therefore, this law is not much better than a policy directive whose implementation is dependent on the whims and caprice of the government.

The Maharashtra Act of 1986 is an improvement on its precursor the Maharashtra Resettlement of Project Displaced Persons Act, 1976 and also, the MP Act for it is automatically applicable to all irrigation projects in which the area of the affected zone exceeds 50 hectares or the area of the benefited zone exceeds 200 hectares or if an entire village (*gaothan*) is affected S. 1 (4). Unfortunately, this Act is not applicable to inter-state projects S. 1 (4) (c). The Act can also be made applicable to non-irrigation projects if the state government thinks that it would be necessary and expedient in the public interest to do so. S. 1 (4) (b).

In 1987 the Karnataka legislature approved the Karnataka Resettlement of Project Displaced Persons Bill. This too is now believed to be awaiting the assent of the President.

In other states the approach to the problem of rehabilitation has been piecemeal. Provisions relating to the rehabilitation of displaced persons are to be found in a host of resolutions, circulars and memos issued by the executive branch of the state government. All these directives are in the nature of policy guidelines that the concerned government department is required to keep in mind while executing a new project. The displaced have no legal right to demand that these guidelines be adhered to and implemented.

A scrutiny of these directives reveals that there is no uniformity with regard to the persons who are entitled to be rehabilitated, the nature of compensation offered, the civic amenities and facilities to be made available at the new site, etc. These policies vary not only across states, but from project to project as well. Indeed, it would not be an exaggeration to say that there are as many policies as there are projects.

Let us briefly review the salient features and shortcomings of these policies.

1. By and large, it is the landholders who are regarded as displaced persons and consequently entitled to such compensation

and relief as may be available under the policy in question. In this respect, the policies of the state governments appear to be based on the principle followed under the Land Acquisition Act of 1894: that only persons who have a direct (owner, joint holders as in the case of a Hindu undivided family) or indirect (a tenant or a mortgagee) interest are considered to be entitled to compensation for the acquisition of their land.

Agricultural labourers who do not own any land but who earn their livelihood principally by manual labour on agricultural land have been regarded as displaced persons by some states like Gujarat and Orissa. But others who belong to the category of the landless (skilled labourers, artisans, craftsmen) do not appear to exist in the eyes of the policy-framers. Plans must be made to provide them with alternate employment or facilities to enable them to continue their current occupations in their new villages. Their lives too will be disrupted as a consequence of the acquisition of land in their village.

2. Another group that is often neglected by the policy-makers is that of women. A scrutiny of the definition of 'displaced person/ oustee' read in conjunction with that of 'family' reveals that in many cases an adult woman who is either unmarried or divorced and who does not hold any land in her own right is neither considered to be a displaced person nor part of the family of such a person! Consequently, she will not be entitled to any relief. What is to become of her?

3. Most policies contain provisions for allotment of alternate agricultural land and house sites to families whose land has been acquired for the project. The basis on which this alternate land is allotted is generally the area of the land lost. Such a policy ignores the fact that submergence of farm land starkly affects the work opportunities for landless agricultural labour and that such families also need to be rehabilitated. Therefore, it may be more equitable to take as the point of departure the post-submergence asset ownership structure of the displaced and build a system of relief around it.

This alternate land is allotted in one of the following ways. The government allows the oustees to search for and find their own land; gives them cash support in accordance with the entitlement of the family at the time of the purchase; or it creates a land pool from government agricultural lands as well as farm lands likely to be sold by farmers in other villages, negotiates the prices with the owners and then offers such land to the oustees at a price determined by it. This is the case in the Sardar Sarovar project in Gujarat.

The policy of offering cash grants and leaving the oustees to find land for themselves is not conducive to the interests of the displaced as it is difficult for individual oustees to negotiate competitive prices. This is particularly so in the case of tribals who tend to get caught in the clutches of exploitative landowners, lawyers and money-lenders.

Further, the assets held by the oustees are generally undervalued by the assessing authority, while the value of the assets in the adjacent areas where the oustees want to move is inflated. Thus, cash grants do not take them very far in the matter of securing alternate land.

The alternate land that is offered by the government is generally poorer in quality than that which has been acquired and may not even be a viable holding. In a few instances provision is made for allotment of alternate agricultural land in the command area of a project.

Keeping in mind the constant and invariable nature of available land, one is led to question the wisdom of the 'land for land' policy. The number of those whom the land has to support and the number of those who desire to acquire land is increasing constantly. Thus, there will come a time when it will not be possible to provide the stipulated amount of land or perhaps any land at all to displaced persons.

The 'land for land' policy suffers from inherent limitations and it is necessary to seek other and more effective modes of rehabilitation.
4. Persons displaced by a project are rarely relocated as communities. Relocation tends to take place on an individual basis for it is far easier to pay individual households and allow them to take care of themselves. More often than not, scant attention is paid to the need to prepare the prospective oustees for displacement *and* ensure their integration into the community. The socio-psychological implications of displacement, particularly relevant in the case of tribals, have been sorely neglected.
5. Neither at the state nor the national level is there any department or authority that deals exclusively with the formulation, implementation and monitoring of rehabilitation programmes. 'While the projects are executed by irrigation, power, mining, forests or other departments, the rehabilitation aspect is handled mostly by the Revenue Department in the states . . . .' As for the

actual implementation of rehabilitation programmes, the machinery generally created at the field level is of an *ad hoc* nature, sporadic and there is no continuing organisation with the required amount of expertise to formulate programmes and monitor their imple-mentation' (Recommendations of the Committee on Rehabilitation of Displaced Tribals Due to Development Projects, Ministry of Home Affairs, Government of India, 1985).

How do the Maharashtra and Madhya Pradesh statutes on the subject of rehabilitation compare with the policies outlined above?

a) The Maharashtra Project—Affected Persons Rehabilitation Act, 1986 (The Maharashtra Act) recognises the landless—(craftsmen, traders, professionals and agricultural labourers who do not own any land) as 'affected persons' entitled to rehabilitation benefits under the Act but the Madhya Pradesh Pariyojana Ke Karan Visthapit Vyakti Punhsthapan Adhiniyam, 1985 (the MP Act) does not. Thus the provisions of the Maharashtra Act are quite salutary but under the MP Act the landless are no better off than those governed by the policy directives of other states.

b) Both Acts treat all women, who are residing with and are dependent on the displaced person for their livelihood, irrespective of their age, as part of the family.

c) Both Acts stipulate that in the case of an irrigation project, subject to be availability of sufficient land, the state government must rehabilitate the displaced persons on land in the villages or areas which will receive the benefit of irrigation from such project. The grant of such alternate agricultural land is, of course, subject to the payment of the stipulated price by such displaced person.

d) Both the Maharashtra and the MP Acts provide for resettle-ment of diplaced persons as a community and have made provision for the constitution of an authority to advise the state government in all matters relating to the resettlement of displaced persons, to implement the resettlement programme and supervise the fieldwork of resettlement and arrange, as far as practicable, for the employ-ment of displaced persons in any work connected with the project or otherwise.

Thus, as regards the nature of the alternate agricultural land offered, the resettlement of displaced persons as a community rather than on an individual basis, and the machinery for supervising the resettlement of these persons, the provisions of the Maha-rashtra and MP statutes are superior to those of most policies formulated by other states.

Rehabilitation Policy of the Central Ministries

The lack of a uniform rehabilitation policy is equally noticeable in cases of acquisition of land by the central government for projects under the Ministries of Energy, Steel and Mines, Industry, Environment and Forests, etc. As in the case of the state government, each of these Ministries has issued various circulars and memos from time to time indicating the policy of facilities to be afforded to persons displaced by its projects.

A notable feature of these directives is that quite a few of them contain provisions for the employment (to the extent possible) of one member of each displaced family, e.g., see the National Thermal Power Corporation Limited's 'Policy on Facilities To Be Given To Land Oustees'—instructions issued periodically by the Bureau of Public Enterprises, Ministry of Industrial Development to public sector undertakings and enterprises regarding preferential treatment in the matter of employment for displaced persons.

The provision of alternative employment or preferential treatment for the displaced in the matter of employment appears to be a better solution than the mere payment of cash compensation for the land acquired. However, a serious effort must be made to impart vocational/technical training necessary to equip the displaced persons who generally belong to the agrarian sector for employment in other fields. Failing this, alternative employment/preferential treatment will not prove to be a very effective means of rehabilitation.

National Policy on Rehabilitation

The inescapable conclusion to be drawn from these facts is that there is a pressing need for the formulation of a policy applicable to the whole country dealing comprehensively with the resettlement and rehabilitation of displaced persons and other related issues. Such a policy should be binding on all the state governments as well as the centre or else they will continue to adopt piecemeal *ad hoc* measures in this regard, particularly when forced to do so by overwhelming public opinion or when the people affected in a particular area are organised enough to form strong pressure groups.

The salient features of such a policy should include:

a) The rehabilitation scheme should be prepared well in advance along with the project report and should form a part of it. The Supreme Court observed in a case involving the acquisition of land by Coal India Limited that:

> before any developmental project is taken up, the social cost involved must be evaluated with a view to balancing the advantages . . . every developmental programme must provide for the simultaneous rehabilitation of the persons who are thrown out of their land and houses on account of acquisition of land for such developmental projects. No developmental project, however laudable, can possibly justify impoverishment of large sections of people and their utter destitution. (*Lalchand Mahto & Ors* vs *Coal India Ltd.* in the Supreme Court of India, Civil Original Jurisdiction, MP No. 16331 of 1982).

Such a scheme should ensure that it provides for preparing the affected groups for transfer to the new site (perhaps with the aid of voluntary social organisations), their systematic mobilisation to the new site and their integration into the host community, which should be conditioned to accept them and not adopt a hostile attitude.

b) The policy should cover all categories of persons who will be affected by the project whether or not they hold any land, i.e., landless labourers, sharecroppers, artisans, nomads, cowherds, forest produce collectors, etc., for the lives of such persons are also totally disrupted when entire villages are acquired. They too are compelled to shift and start afresh as a result of the acquisition and though not landholders, they are an integral part of the social and economic fabric of the village community and their claim to rehabilitation should definitely be taken into account.

c) Cash compensation alone is clearly inadequate. Therefore, this needs to be buttressed by other rehabilitative measures to ensure that the displaced have an assured source of income: training programmes in various trades, crafts and professions to enable landless or other oustees, particularly the youth, to enter the non-agrarian sector; preferential treatment in the matter of employment on the project and in government service; assistance to displaced persons to set up small-scale industries and ancillary units in the vicinity of the project area.

Where cash compensation is given, there should be adequate safeguards to ensure that it is not misused or squandered.

d) There should be provision for alternate agricultural land to those who desire compensation in this form. However, this should certainly not be the sole rehabilitative measure for, given the limited quantity of land available, how long can this be considered an effective means of rehabilitation? Would it not be better to offer them an option in the form of education and technical training to equip them to become a part of the ever-expanding non-agrarian sector?

e) This brings us to the need to make provision for the compulsory education of children as also adult education. The role played by women in the rural economy should be recognised and rural development programmes with a focus on women should be implemented. The interests of children find no place in the existing rehabilitation schemes nor do those of women as a separate group.

f) Group as opposed to individual rehabilitation should be the norm. This is particularly important in the case of tribals to ensure that the disruptive consequences of displacement are kept to the minimum.

g) There should be a separate Ministry or Authority of Rehabilitation, perhaps for each state, with the purpose of formulating and implementing rehabilitation programmes while adhering to certain basic principles uniformly applicable to all projects. This will ensure that rehabilitation programmes are not given the niggardly treatment they receive today.

h) Though the policy should be a national one in the sense that it will be applicable to the whole of India, it must be flexible enough to accomodate changes that may need to be made in it on account of circumstances peculiar to a particular project or the conditions existing in a given region. Given the diversity of the Indian situation, no one policy can possibly cater to the varied needs of the particular region in which a project may be situated.

Rehabilitation is a delicate task requiring a good deal of understanding and dedication. Therefore, the need of the hour is for a comprehensive and legally binding policy on the subject, along with officials who are motivated and genuinely interested in implementing such a policy. The one will be ineffective without the other.

References

Annual Survey of Indian Law. 1987. Volume XXIII. Indian Law Institute. 154.
Government of India. 1985. *Report of Committee on Rehabilitation of Displaced Tribals Due to Development Projects*. New Delhi: Ministry of Home Affairs.
Maradi, M., P.J. Nayak and R.S. Patil. 1989. *Reservoir Submergence and Rehabilitation: Six Villages in the Upper Krishna Project*. Bangalore.

8

Evaluating Major Irrigation Projects in India

SHEKHAR SINGH • ASHISH KOTHARI •
KULAN AMIN

Cost-Benefit Analysis Method

The task of evaluating major irrigation projects has always been
fraught with uncertainties. Traditionally, to establish the financial
and economic viability of such projects, a financial and economic
cost-benefit analysis was carried out. The Planning Commission
laid down that only those projects would be considered for approval
whose cost-benefit ratio was not below 1: 1.5. However, in the last
few years, this method of evaluation, especially the manner in
which it has been applied by project authorities, has lost credibility.

Note: The following persons helped in the writing of this paper and the compilation
of information on which this paper is based. Their contribution is gratefully ack-
nowledged: Niti Anand, Miloon Kothari, Raman Mehta, Rachanaa Maheshwari,
Rupa Desai and Satyajit Singh. Comments on an earlier draft of this paper by Alan
Rodgers, Kamal Kabra, Chiranjeev Bedi, Nandan Maluste, Pranab Banerji and
Saumitra Chowdhry, have been most helpful in saving us from many errors. An
earlier version of this paper was presented to the Fellows of the Indian Academy of
Sciences, at a meeting at the Indian Institute of Science, Bangalore, in August
1989.

In addition, there has been an increasing demand to evaluate the social impact of projects as well, including their impact on the environment, and on the lives of people such projects invariably render homeless—the oustees.

The experience of people affected by projects in the past has been very unpleasant, to say the least, and this has led, perhaps for the first time, to a scrutiny by individuals and organisations outside the government, of irrigation project reports and their anticipated costs and benefits.

The cost-benefit method of evaluating major dams is being questioned today primarily for three reasons. First, a scrutiny of past projects has shown that even those cost and benefits which are easily quantifiable and therefore easily anticipated within the traditional, financial and economic framework, have often been wrongly estimated. The Public Accounts Committee of the Parliament stated that a scrutiny of 32 major projects in post-independence India has shown cost overruns of 500 per cent and more. Not only have the costs been underestimated, the benefits have also been exaggerated.

Second, it has now been recognised that there are additional costs of such projects which have not been taken into consideration in the cost-benefit analysis. The most significant among these are the suffering of displaced families and the impact on the environment. It is now generally accepted that it would be impossible to measure these in purely financial or economic terms.

Third, although no retrospective cost-benefit analysis has been made of the major dams in India, a comparison of their actual and anticipated cost-benefit from available studies of some projects (quoted later) suggest that most of these projects have had higher costs than benefits, and certainly a cost-benefit ratio inferior to what was anticipated or required. This has resulted in the conviction that dams must be evaluated in a wider and more realistic perspective.

This paper is an attempt towards building a broader perspective by discussing the evidence available on these projects, especially on their costs and benefits.It presents a retrospective analysis of major dams in India, based on data gleaned from official documents: primarily reports of the Public Accounts Committee, the Comptroller and Auditor General of India, Committees of Ministry of Irrigation, project reports and other documents pertaining to different projects.

The Context of Evaluation

While evaluating dams one has to consider at least the following aspects:

THE PLANNING PROCESS

The socio-economic reality of the potential command area has to be studied, identifying the primary needs of the area and the region, and the possible alternative methods of satisfying these. For example, there might be poverty and unemployment in an area, but for various reasons the best strategy for alleviating these might not be a promotion of agricuture but the development of an artisanal and rural industrial base.

Where the best option turns out to be the development of agriculture, it is necessary to evaluate whether this should be irrigated agriculture or rainfed dry land farming, or a mixture of the two.

Where irrigated agriculture emerges as the best prospect, it must again be analysed whether this should be through utilisation of ground water, minor irrigation schemes, drip irrigation, or through the building of large dams. A thorough analysis involves the investigation of all possibilities.

COST-BENEFIT ANALYSIS

If a major dam is initially considered the best alternative, a detailed cost-benefit analysis has to be made, which must realistically establish that the benefits from the project are greater than the costs.

Such an exercise includes financial, economic and social costing.

A Financial Cost-benefit Analysis: only considers the purely monetary costs to be incurred by the project, such as the cost of cement, steel and labour for the construction of the dam and canals. Where land has to be acquired, the monetary price of this land is also included in such an exercise. Similarly, it takes into account the monetary benefits flowing to the project, for instance, the water rates collected, or revenue earned through sale of electricity.

An Economic Cost-benefit Analysis: considers the economic costs of the project which are to be borne by society, for example, the loss of produce from land to be submerged, or the economic loss of fisheries, or timber and firewood, even though this is *not* a monetary outflow from the project. Among benefits it would consider the economic benefits of enhanced crop production, even though this does not represent a monetary inflow to the project.

The Social Cost-benefit Analysis: calculates the non-economic costs and benefits of a project, for example, the dislocation and suffering of the people who have been ousted. It similarly calculates the non-economic benefits, such as, the benefits from drinking water. A social cost-benefit analysis also includes an environmental impact assessment, for instance, the biological loss due to submergence of forests or the biological benefit of a freshwater reservoir.

All these aspects of analysis together make for the ability to appraise a given project, and to compare it with other possible projects which have been similarly analysed. It is therefore essential, in order to evaluate a project, that alternatives to the project under consideration be adequately studied in order to arrive at the optimum investment choice.

While conducting a cost-benefit analysis, it has to be ensured that *all* the quantifiable financial, economic, and social costs and benefits are computed realistically.

Next, the project has to be implemented in as short a time as possible, and certainly within the stipulated period, to ensure that the benefits become available as soon as possible and that the costs remain within the levels anticipated.

RETROSPECTIVE COST-BENEFIT ANALYSIS

To verify the accuracy of cost-benefit projections, it is necessary to look at these projects in retrospect and evaluate whether they were completed within the stipulated costs and are giving the projected benefits, and if not, the reasons why.

CLASS-BENEFIT ANALYSIS

In India, with its stark social and economic disparities, there is an avowed commitment to equity and socialism. The Constitution of

India, for example, describes the nation as a 'sovereign, democratic, socialist republic'. It is therefore not enough for a project to have benefits greater than costs; it must be ensured that the benefits of the project accrue primarily to the poor, while the costs are borne primarily by the rich. In any case, the converse is certainly not justifiable.

The Situation Today

COST-BENEFIT ANALYSIS

Cost Over-runs: Although no definitive data on the amount invested in major dam projects since Independence are available, it is estimated that between 30 to 40 thousand crores, at current prices, has so far been invested in this sector. It is interesting to see how efficiently this money has been spent.

Fact 1: 32 major on-going and initiated projects (Fifth and Sixth Plans) studied by the Public Accounts Committee (PAC) show cost overruns of 500 per cent or more (PAC 1982–83: 38).

Fact 2: No project has been completed within the approved cost estimates since Independence (PAC 1982–83: 1).

Acknowledging this, the Ministry of Irrigation reported to the PAC that during the Seventh Plan they would only support medium and minor projects and concentrate on completing all existing projects (PAC 1986–87: 100).

It is true that when a project is delayed, some of the cost increases are due to inflation and do not constitute a real increase in the cost of the project. However, considering the actual cost overruns of projects in India, only a very small proportion of these can be attributed to inflation. Even a delay of 15 years in completing the project would inflate the cost by only 150 per cent (at 8.5 per cent inflation rate per annum) and not by 500 per cent.

Time Overruns: Not only are time overruns one reason for cost overruns, but they also delay the benefits of the projects from reaching the people, sometimes indefinitely. They adversely affect the cost-benefit ratios and it can be argued that projects which are delayed beyond a certain period are no longer economically viable.

Considering that the returns of a project are calculated on the basis of returns on the investment, the opportunity cost of delayed returns is very high and can make the project economically non-viable even with a delay of a few years. In the case of the Sardar Sarovar project, for example, the World Bank conducted a sensitivity analysis to assess how sensitive the project was to certain variables. They determined that a delay in implementation of 22 per cent (five years for this project) would reduce the present value of the net benefits to zero (Paranjpye 1989).

Fact 1: Of the 205 major projects taken up since Independence, ony 29 had been completed till 1979–80 (PAC 1982–83: 48, para 2.49).

Fact 2: Not a single project has been completed, since Independence, within the stipulated target dates (PAC 1982–83: 1, para 1.1).

The Naegamwala Committee (Naegamwala 1973), and a working group constituted by the Planning Commission have identified the following reasons for delays in projects:

(i) Proliferation of projects under construction by the states, resulting in a thin spread of financial, managerial and technical resources.

(ii) Large escalations in costs of projects which were found to occur due to large-scale increases in cost of labour, materials, equipment, spares, land, etc.

(iii) Lack of thorough investigations prior to taking up the projects.

(iv) Delays in taking important decisions.

(v) Difficulties in land acquisition.

(vi) Non-availability of scarce materials like cement, steel, explosives, machinery, spares and foreign exchange.

(vii) Changes in scope of projects during implementation due to inadequate planning, including addition of drainage arrangements and flood protecting to command areas.

(viii) Lack of construction planning and monitoring organisations.

(ix) Lack of detailed plans and estimates for the distribution systems and structure thereon.

(x) Failure to update estimates in time and keep state governments informed of the rise in costs of projects.

Looking at Alternatives

One of the most disturbing aspects of the planning of major dams in India is the almost total lack of attention to alternatives that might exist or could be developed. Not only could there be alternative designs to a project which could minimise the cost (as has been suggested in the case of Narmada Sagar and Sardar Sarovar), there could also be alternatives to major dams themselves.

One of the alternatives that has not been adequately promoted is minor irrigation. The PAC report of 1982–83, quoting from the *Economic Survey* of the Planning Commission, says. 'Minor irrigation projects cost much less and promote rural capital formation because a part of the investment is funded through the farmers' own savings. Time-lag between investment decision and the flow of benefits is comparatively small' (PAC 1982–83: 29, para 2.29).

The PAC records: 'In any case, drought conditions call for quick result-yielding schemes which is possible only through development of minor irrigation facilities' (PAC 1982–83: 171).

Apart from minor irrigation, many other types of alternatives exist which include use of ground water and sprinklers, drip irrigation, lift irrigation, etc. In the context of arid and semi-arid areas like Gujarat and Rajasthan, it is interesting to note that the PAC, in its report of 1986–87 says, 'The drip method of irrigation has been found to be very useful in reclaiming and developing the Arava desert area in Israel . . . We have large areas in our country which are arid or semi-arid, with problems similar to those in Israel' (PAC 1986–87: 57–58, para 6.42).

Generally speaking, the PAC takes the view that adequate research is not being done to identify and develop alternatives even though such alternatives have shown very promising results in other countries and would save much cost and minimise environmental degradation.

As far back as 1972, the Irrigation Commission had recommended that 'the basin plan should present a comprehensive outline of development possiblities of land and water resources to meet the anticipated regional and local needs '(quoted in PAC 1986–87: 43, para 19.11). The PAC goes on to say, 'There should be a number of fully investigated schemes kept ready for choice, so that financial resources may not get deployed on relatively uneconomic schemes. The quality of investigations should not be sacrificed to speed up project formulation' (PAC 1987–88: 51).

Ignoring Several Cost Factors

It has already been mentioned that studies on the impact of river valley projects on the environment were not undertaken until this decade. According to the Planning Commission, 'of course environmental impact studies have not been carried out in any of the projects so far' (PAC 1982–82: 8, para 2.5).

Even environmental costs are not adequately computed or considered in the cost-benefit analysis. Though this is partly due to the difficulty in computing some of these costs in financial and economic terms, a more important reason is the hesitation on the part of project authorities to acknowledge these costs. There is also a general lack of sensitivity to environmental issues.

Another cost that is usually underestimated is that of properly rehabilitating those displaced by the project. This not only distorts the cost-benefit analysis but also implies grave hardships for the displaced families.

A cost that is even today not properly computed in a cost-benefit analysis is that of the waterlogging and salinity caused by the project. Though this has been recognised for many years as a major negative effect of irrigation projects in India, the Secretary, Ministry of Irrigation, Government of India, admitted to the PAC that, 'After all, some items are not provided for in the original estimates. It so happens, for instance, drainage is not provided for in many projects' (PAC 1982–82: 60).

The CAG, in his report for 1979–80 for Madhya Pradesh, made the following observations regarding Tawa dam, the first major dam to be built in the Narmada Valley:

> The Table given below shows the comparative position of the yields per acre under various crops after irrigation during 1977–78 and 1978–79 and the yields prior to introduction of irrigation (1971–72) in Hoshangabad district, as per the Agricultural Statistics compiled by the Commissioner. Land Records.

Crop	Before irrigation	Average yields per acre after irrigation	
		1977–78	1978–79
		(in quintals)	
1. Paddy	4.00	2.98	3.83
2. Jowar	2.82	3.64	2.74
3. Maize	4.81	4.07	4.01
4. Wheat	3.14	3.30	3.06
5. Gram	2.43	1.96	2.08

It will be noticed that the yields per acre after irrigation had actually declined.

According to the scientific and technical opinion now available, because of the soil and weather conditions in the command area of the Tawa project, agricultural operations in both kharif and rabi seasons with the help of irrigation could not have been productive, but on the other hand, irrigation could be even harmful. There was also resistance on the part of cultivators to a change in their habits and the cropping pattern they have been used to. Thus, it would appear that the project was ill-concieved and the benefits that were presumed would be available could not have been realised. (CAG 1979–80)

The PAC report of 1986–87 once again reiterates these fears:

In irrigation projects due attention should be paid to the drainage problems of the command area, to avoid waterlogging and its attendant evil, salt efflorescence. In some of our earlier irrigation projects, the aspect had been neglected with the result that hundreds of thousands of hectares of irrigated land have been damaged or rendered completely unfit for cultivation. (PAC 1986–87: 49, para 5.36)

OVERESTIMATION OF BENEFITS

Shortfall in Utilising Irrigation Potential: An analysis of some of the major dams reveals interesting figures concerning the shortfall in the utilisation of irrigation potential.

The Comptroller and Auditor General of India, in the supplementary report for 1975–76, studied 12 major projects and came to the conclusion that the area actually irrigated was on average only 64.4 per cent of the area planned to be irrigated. Even this average is misleading as there were five among these 12, where the irrigated area was less than 40 per cent and one with less than 20 per cent of that anticipated (see Table 8.1).

TABLE 8.1

Name of the Project	Area planned to be irrigated	Average area irrigated in 5 years	Percentage of achievement over expectation
	(in thousand hectares)		
Bhakra Nangal			
Punjab	433.4	284.8	65.7
Haryana	717.1	869.7	121.3
Rajasthan	231.0	266.6	115.4
Chambal			
Madhya Pradesh	273.3	134.5	49.2
Rajasthan	283.5	164.8	58.1
Sardar Canal System			
Uttar Pradesh	1100.2	848.2	77.1
Kosi Eastern Main Canal and Rajpur Branch Canal			
Bihar	743.7	135.1	18.2
Hirakud Orrisa	249.4	240.9	96.6
Mayurakshi West Bengal	289.5	217.4	75.1
Tungabhadra Karnataka (B)	353.8	209.3	59.2
Right Bank Low Level Canal			
Andhra Pradesh	60.2	39.5	65.6
Nagarjunasagar Andhra Pradesh (C)	831.6	322.6	38.8
Parambikulam Aliyar			
Tamil Nadu	101.5	30.1	29.7
Kakrapar Gujarat	256.0	84.1	32.9
Purna Maharashtra	62.0	24.7	39.8
Girna Maharashtra	57.2	22.3	39.0
Total	6043.4	3894.6	64.4

Source: Adapted from CAG 1975–76: 23–24.

Transmission Loss of Water: Another parameter crucial in evaluating the benefits of dams is the transmission loss of water, sometimes causing waterlogging. Again, no detailed figures are available but the Public Accounts Committee, quoting the Comptroller and Auditor General's supplementary report of 1975–76, has stated that the difference between projected and observed losses has been around 150 to 300 per cent, in one case going up to nearly 500 per cent (see Table 8.2).

TABLE 8.2

Canal	Losses projected	Losses observed	Difference between observed and projected losses (cusecs/million sft)	Losses observed as percentage of losses projected
Chambal Right Main Canal	8	15	7	187.5
Tawa	8	22.8	14.8	285.0
Mahanadi Canal System (MP)	8	39.7	31.7	496.2
Nagarjunasagar Left Bank Canal	8	21.2	13.2	265.0
Nagarjunasagar Right Bank Canal	8	16.7	8.7	208.7
Periyar Main Canal (Lined)	2	3.5	1.5	175.0
Periyar Branch Canals (Lined)	2	3.25	1.25	162.5
Periyar Branch Canals (Lined)	2	3.26	1.26	163.0
Periyar Vaigai Distribute and Water Courses (unlined)	8	2.7	5.3	33.7
Girna/Jamda LBC	8	11.0	3.0	137.5
Mula Right Bank Canal	8	24–25	16–17	300–312.5
Nira Right Bank Canal	8	6.0	−2.0	75.0
Purna (Bamath Branch)	8	15.0	7.0	187.5
Mula Sonai Distributary	8	9–19	1–11	112.5–237.5

Source: PAC 1982–83: 100.[1]

Siltation: The benefits of a project depend a great deal on the life of the project. Siltation of reservoirs significantly reduces their life and sometimes even their safety. The most effective method of controlling siltation rates of reservoirs is by treating the catchment areas. The construction of dams invariably degrades the catchment areas as pressures supported by the land and forests that are submerged by the project, get transferred partly or wholly to the remaining land and forest in the catchment area. In its turn this degradation negatively affects the dam and the reservoir.

Many estimates show that the rate of siltation in most of our reservoirs is much higher than that anticipated, in many cases over 400 per cent more than anticipated. In one case, Nizamsagar, the rate of siltation is 1,642 per cent higher than anticipated (see Tables 8.3 and 8.4).

TABLE 8.3

Name of reservoir	Annual rate of siltation (ha m/1000 sq km)		Percentage of assumed life actually available*
	Assumed	Observed	
Bhakra	4.29	5.95	72.2
Tungabhadra	4.29	5.98	78.77
Matatila	1.33	4.33	30.25
Panchet	6.67	10.48	63.88
Maithon	9.05	12.39	72.85
Mayurakshi	3.75	16.48	22.70
Shivaji Sagar	6.67	15.24	44
Hirakud	2.52	6.6	38.087
Gandhi Sagar	3.61	9.64	37.41

Source: Adapted from PAC 1982–83: 103.
* Life of reservoir refers to physical life based on the rates of siltation assumed at the design stage and presently observed

TABLE 8.4

Reservoir	Annual rate of siltation in acre ft.		Percentage difference between observed and assumed siltation rate
	Assumed	Observed	
Bhakra	23,000	33,745	146.7
Maithon (DVC)	684	5,980	874.2
Panchet (DVC)	1,982	9,533	480.9
Ramganga	1,089	4,366	400.9
Tungabhadra	9,796	41,058	419.1
Mayurakshi	538	2,000	371.7
Nizam Sagar	530	8,725	1,646.2
Ukai	7,448	21,758	292.1

Source: ICR 1972, Vol. I: 326, Table 14.1.

Recovery of Water Rates: One of the factors in calculating the benefits of major irrigation projects are financial returns obtained from these projects by way of recovery of water rates. However, despite these being shown as a surplus in all cost-benefit analyses, the actual situation is somewhat different. The PAC has the following to say:

> In 1945–46, i.e., just before Independence, the return from irrigation schemes was Rs 7.92 crores on an investment of Rs 149 crores, i.e., 5.3 per cent. This came down to Rs 1 crore in the following year and thereafter the irrigation and multi purpose projects have been consistantly showing losses. These have mounted from nearly Rs 154.6 crores in 1975–76 to Rs 424.75 crores in 1981–82 (budget estimates), both in respect of irrigation (commercial) and multi purpose river valley projects. (PAC 1982–83: 135, para 4.39)

> The Fifth Five Year Plan document had pointed out that in certain states, receipts from irrigation were not sufficient even to cover the working expenses and this in fact amounted to subsidising of farmers, rather the relatively better-off farmers . . . . The Committee find that the cumulative losses were of the order of Rs 2,053 crores between 1975–76 and 1981–82. Obviously, this situation cannot and should not be allowed to continue. (PAC 1982–83: 135–136, para 4.40)

RETROSPECTIVE COST-BENEFIT ANALYSIS

It seems incredible that despite the huge investment made on major dams in India there has been little effort at evaluating the actual returns from these projects and comparing these to the projected returns. The Planning Commission admits that 'there is no regular system of assessing actual economic returns of irrigation projects' (PAC 1982–83: 114).

The PAC states that:

> The Committee are surprised to learn that net increase in yield in the command of an irrigation project is not assessed. In the absence of such an assessment the Committee wonders how actual benefit derived could be ascertained and compared with the project anticipation. Henceforth such data should be compiled regularly. (PAC 1982–83: 124, para 4.25)

The PAC further recommends that:

In future the Planning Commission should therefore undertake a detailed appraisal of implementation of plans, inter-alia
bringing out the physical and financial targets and achievements and reasons for the shortfall in achievements as well as
the deficiencies in implementation during the mid-term and
after every five year plan to apply on-course corrections and
formulate the next plan in the light of these. These detailed
appraisal reports should be made public. (PAC 1982–83: 146,
para 6.10)

Class-Benefit Analysis

In virtually every project it is seen that the primary costs are being
paid by the very poor and the tribals, while the benefits are flowing
to big farmers and the urban elite. Those who are displaced by
such projects are usually too poor and politically weak to safe
guard their own interests. The government has little difficulty in
imposing its will on such people. However, when it comes to
finding suitable alternative land for the displaced, the government
seems to lack the political will required to ensure that good cultivable lands are made available. To resettle families to be dislocated
by the Sardar Sarovar project, the Maharashtra government is
now insisting that forest land be made available. In most projects,
current and past, the authorities have been unwilling to make the
rich farmers who would benefit from the project, share some of
these benefits with those who would be uprooted.

As already mentioned, even in fixing and recovering water
rates, the govenment is socially remiss. The PAC in its report has
the following to say:

> In their earlier recommendation the Committee had speci-
> fically observed that they saw no reason why the big land
> owners who were the principal beneficiaries of the irrigation
> facility should continue to be subsidised and desired that this
> matter should be thrashed out at the next Conference of
> Chief Ministers so that the oft-repeated exhortations of the
> planners were translated into action without further loss of
> time. The Committee note that the government have merely
> stated that the states have necessarily to raise the irrigation

rates with a view to covering at least the working expenses and have not examined the aforesaid recommendations of the Committee relating to big land owners. The Committee are unable to understand this. There is no warrant for the big land owners who are the principal beneficiaries of the irrigation facilities to continue to be subsidised in respect of water rates. (PAC 1986–87: 139)

Planning Process

The fact that such a situation exists in India today is necessarily a reflection of the planning process out of which such projects emerge, are appraised and evaluated. Recorded below are some of the relevant observations made by the CAG and the PAC about the planning process in India.

1. For no major irrigation project in India has a study been conducted to establish, step by step, that such a project is the best choice for the region and its problems.

2. Though there have been repeated demands, to date no state has prepared the required Master Plans for water management. The PAC had this to say:

> The Committee in their earlier report had pointed out that one of the strategies/priorities of the Sixth Five Year Plan, in the irrigation sector, had been the preparation of Statewise Master Plans and completion of all investigations by 1989–90. However, not a single state had prepared such a plan pending completion of investigations needed thereof . . . . The Committee are unable to comprehend the reasons for not expediting the investigations and preparations of Master Plans. (PAC 1986–87: 135–36)

3. Lack of comprehensive planning, and the absence of an adequate National Water Utilisation Plan, built on the basis of state management plans, has led to the proliferation of projects and the subsequent shortage of funds and other inputs. The PAC observes:

The Committee, therefore, consider it to be a negation of planning for the Planning Commission to sanction a large number of major schemes without making sure of the availability of funds, the technical personnel and essential inputs like cement, steel, coal etc. to enable completion of the projects within the time schedule laid down and within the approved estimates. (PAC 1982–83: 171)

4. Another distortion in the planning process occurs when projects are begun before clearence is given by the Planning Commission and other relevant authorities. This not only subverts the process of project appraisal, aimed at selecting only beneficial projects, but also puts pressure on the various authorities to grant *post-facto* clearance for such projects. Even for those projects which can be shown to be economically non-viable, considering the huge amounts of money already spent prior to the clearance, it becomes uneconomical and politically difficult to abandon them. Table 8.5 shows the record of certain past projects.

TABLE 8.5

Name of scheme	Date of approval by Planning Com- mission/Ministry of Irrigation	Date of commencement of work
1. Nagarjunasagar (Andhra Pradesh)	22-9-60	1955
2. Rajasthan Canal Project (Rajasthan)		
Stage I	4-7-57	1958
Stage II	17-5-72	1972
3. Gandak (Bihar)	13-7-61	1961
4. Kosi (Bihar)	25-4-58	1955
5. Malaprabha (Karnataka)	5-8-63	Oct. 1960
6. Kallda (Kerala)	4/7-2-66	1966
7. Tawa (MP)	5-8-60	1956
8. Kangasabati (West Bengal)	28-11-61	1956

Source: (PAC 1982–83: 42).

The Public Accounts Committee has observed:

The Committee find that in several cases the approval by the Planning Commission/Ministry of Irrigation was accorded three to five years after commencement of work. Irrigation being a state subject and central assistance not being tied to any individual project or sector, the states are reported to commence work on some irrigation projects on their own. However, plan allocation of funds for any such unapproved projects is on the stipulation that the project would be cleared by the Planning Commission. The tendency to take up too many projects without getting prior clearance of the Planning Commission/Ministry of Irrigation amounts to pre-empting such clearance. It was conceded in evidence that there should be certain discipline and proper procedure in regard to these things. The Committee considered that any ad-hocism in project selection could be a self-defeating exercise. (PAC 1982–83: 171)

Conclusions

Given these facts, it is essential that before embarking upon any new project we must:

1. Carry out a retrospective cost-benefit analysis to determine, at least for a sample of our major projects, how beneficial they have been to the country.

2. Examine the reasons why the costs were higher and the benefits lower than anticipated, if the analysis establishes this.

3. Ensure that the new projects are so planned and implemented that this does not recur.

4. Ensure that all the costs and benefits are realistically considered before a project is approved.

5. Ensure that all the alternatives are also properly evaluated so that the country has the benefit of the best of these.

6. Ensure that the projects are socially just.

References

CAG. 1975–76. *Supplementary Report of the Comptroller and Auditor General of India for the Year 1975–76*. Union Government (Civil).

CAG. 1979–80. *Abstract from the Report of the Comptroller and Auditor General of India for the Year 1979–80*. Government of Madhya Pradesh (Civil).

ICR. 1972. *Irrigation Committee Report*. Government of India.

Kothari, A. and S.Singh. 1988. *The Narmada Valley Project: A Critique*. New Delhi: Kalpvriksh.

Naegamvala Report. 1973. *Rise in Costs of Irrigation and Multipurpose Projects*. Report of the Expert Committee, Ministry of Irrigation and Power, Government of India, New Delhi, April.

PAC. 1982–83. Hundred and Forty First Report, Public Accounts Committee, Seventh Lok Sabha. *Planning Process and Monitoring Mechanism with Reference to Irrigation Projects*. Ministry of Planning (Planning Commission), Lok Sabha Secretariat, New Delhi, April, 1983.

PAC. 1986–87. Eighty First Report, Public Accounts Committee, Eighth Lok Sabha, *Planning Process and Monitoring Mechanism with Reference to Irrigation Projects*. Ministry of Planning (Planning Commission), Action taken on the 141st Report (Seventh Lok Sabha), Lok Sabha Secretariat, New Delhi, April, 1987.

Paranjpye, V. 1989. *The Narmada Valley Projects: A Holistic Evaluation of the Sardar Sarovar and Indira (Narmada) Sagar Dams*. INTACH.

9

A Long Long Way from Home: The Search for a Rehabilitation Policy

VASUDHA DHAGAMWAR

Not so very long ago, dams were eulogised as modern temples. As children we saw news reels of the inaugurations of dams. These followed a set pattern. The first shot showed a gnarled, bare-bodied, poor peasant. Ramu bhaiya looked up from the parched ground to scan the cloudless skies above. Would the rains come? Would his crop survive? Would his cattle live? He did not know, said the narrator. His forefathers had not known either. It all rested with his *Kismet*, his fate. But, said the faceless voice with cheer and confidence, this would all be changed. The camera then panned across to the dam. Beaming thousands sat on it, excitedly awaiting the arrival of the dignitary, usually the Prime Minister. The huge expanse of the lake glinted in the background. Even as we were given the vital statistics of the dam, the Prime Minister strode up to cut the tape, pull the switch, open the floodgates. Electricity flowed into the cables and water flowed down the river-bed. India was going modern. India was going to be prosperous. Back to the old gnarled peasant, this time happiness writ large upon his face. Ramu bhaiya would never have to look up at the sky again, the buoyant voice informed us. The dam had saved him. *Jai Hind*.

No one ever asked who had lived on the land that now formed

the vast lake. Where were they now? What were they doing? Did the water really reach Ramu bhaiya or did the rich farmers corner it all? Who got the electricity? Did Ramu bhaiya's village see any of it, leave alone Ramu bhaiya?

Damodar Valley Corporation (DVC) dams in Bihar, Hirakud in Orissa, Bhakra in Punjab, Pong in Himachal, Ukai in Gujarat, Nagarjuna in Andhra Pradesh, Koyna in Maharashtra, Rihand in UP—all these and others came up in the 1950s and 1960s. They offered the solution to our poverty or so everyone, or nearly everyone, said. To be fair, even then there were a few muted voices who challenged the claims made on behalf of dams, who presaged waterlogging, floods, salination. The damage to wildlife and destruction of human habitats did not, however, feature in the arguments. No one was in a mood to listen. From Aswan in Egypt to the DVC in India, cautions were given but to no avail. It must have been bitter satisfaction to those Cassandras when they were later proved right.

Slowly, the voices that expressed doubts about the claims made in favour of dams became louder and more numerous. Experience showed that dams were more expensive and less beneficial than declared. They made the rich richer and the poor poorer. The canals that were to take water hundreds of miles away were rarely completed. Electricity was lost in transmission, floods continued to ravage the land, the water level in the dams was abysmally low.

The last to speak up, as is almost always the case, were the persons most affected—the oustees or people displaced from the submergence areas. In the euphoric past they too had given up all for the larger good of the nation. They took whatever was offered and moved out. Sometimes it was money, sometimes land. If they were not happy with what they were given, or with the brusque, overbearing manner in which they were treated, and the unfeeling manner in which they were driven out, they suffered it all in silence. And they *were* pushed around. The oustees of Pong in hilly Himachal Pradesh were sent off to the faraway desert of Rajasthan. Gujarat procured the submergence area under Ukai from Maharashtra and rehabilitated the Marathi Bhils in Gujarat. Slowly tales of hostile reception by the local populations also began to increase. The oustees did not feel at home, many even fled the new settlements. The land provided was too little, or of poor quality. There was no grazing land, no forest for fuel or fodder. The worst was still to come in the shape of repeated displacement. In the wake of hydroelectric projects came more 'development'. Factories, mines, agro-industries, roads and railways came up and the oustees were displaced several times over. If coal was found near the dam—as it was in Rihand—there was no end to their woes.

If land for land proved to be inappropriate rehabilitation, money compensation provided no rehabilitation at all. It ran through their inexperienced hands like water from a sieve.

In every case the tribals suffered even more as their entire ethos was irrevocably destroyed.

At long last the oustees began to ask, why is it always the poor, the tribals, the villagers who must sacrifice? Why should it always be us? Why do others always gain at our expense? Why don't we get a share in the new riches?

What has only now begun to emerge in India has been happening elsewhere. Opposition to large dams is a worldwide phenomenon. One undeniable gain of all these anti-development agitations and movements has been the increase in the level of public consciousness throughout the world about the human, environmental and ecological costs involved. International funding agencies like the World Bank have gone so far as to create a separate department for resettlement and rehabilitation of the people displaced by projects funded by them.

As their problems were better understood, and the history of past projects became better known, the demands on the behalf of oustees began to be more specific. Money compensation was totally unsatisfactory. It disappeared in a trice and made beggars of men. What they wanted was:

Irrigated land for land.
Land for the landless.
Land for major sons.
Land which satisfied fuel, fodder and timber needs.
Land which allowed continuation of the same life style, especially for tribals who were dependent on forests.
Land in command area.
Houses in keeping with the old life style.
Transport, subsidies, grants, loans.

The one thing they did not ask for was education and training to help them adapt to their changed environs.

The public sector giant steel plants, the industrial townships, the new ports and industries were all similarly greeted by the government, the media and the public as harbingers of a new era. They too displaced thousands but not on such a large-scale. The public did not remember these oustees either, and the government treated their problem with the same thoughtlessness.

If an industry was being set up, jobs were first seen as viable rehabilitation. But it was soon found that the 'one job per family' norm led to fights amongst brothers. At the same time, lack of education made it impossible for the oustees to take on skilled jobs. With bitterness they saw outsiders step into the better paid, high status jobs, while they could only become peons and labourers. The bitterness soon turned to hostility and opposition. Not jobs for land, but land for land.

The central and state governments in India have given very little thought to rehabilitation. A Detailed Project Report of a dam or a steel plant runs into several volumes, but seldom are more than a few pages devoted to the displaced persons and their fate. However, once popular consciousness about their plight began to grow, governments began to make promises which echoed the demands of the activists and the people and assured land to the displaced population. Under pressure, the definition of oustees was enlarged to include major sons, encroachers, and even the landless. The most meaningful and significant change has been the shift in nomenclature to Project Affected Persons—a term far wider than oustees. If all my customers or neighbours are displaced, what good is it for me, though not an oustee, to stay? I am a project affected person and need rehabilitation as much as they do.

But the governments soon began to fight shy of implementing their enthusiastic promises. With respect to Narmada, the most publicised and well-known agitation today, the MP government has made absolutely *no* effort to show land to its oustees. Instead, it points a finger at Gujarat. This, despite the fact that the oustees have a clear right to remain in their own state. The government of Maharashtra is only marginally better. It made *some* effort to identify alternate land, but has now declared that there is no land—neither government land which can be released, nor private land that can be acquired under ceiling laws. It too is urging the oustees to go to Gujarat.

Past experience, present frustrations and future uncertainties have contributed to unite people and activists to proclaim strongly, 'no development at any price'. They are all ranged on one side, irrespective of the project.

On the other side is the government, committed to providing cheap electricity, plentiful water, industrial development and national prosperity. The irresistible force is all set to meet the immovable object.

The activists and the oustees of development projects are openly pitted against the government, opposing dams and development. We are naturally, almost instinctively, inclined to support the people in any campaign against the government, especially when it comes to large-scale, irrevocable and disastrous exploitation of natural resources. So far so good.

But only so far. It is not only to persons displaced by dams or other development projects that the governments have been promising land. This promise is made to others as well—liberated bonded labourers, discharged soldiers, the handicapped and people affected by a calamity, to mention a few. Non-humans have *their* claims on land as well and so do environmental considerations. Witness the schemes for afforestation and wildlife sanctuaries.

What do we say when land is required for rehabilitating bonded labourers? Or when land is needed for afforestation or wildlife sanctuaries? Yet, there are people who are pitted against these activities. Instances of clashing interests are legion. When the declawed, defanged and blind Munna, the dancing bear, was taken away from his owners, they raised the slogan 'man is more important than environment'. Felling of trees is allegedly proceeding apace in Bastar forest as well as Kanha and Kaziranga sanctuaries because villagers and tribals need more land to till. Villagers on the fringes of wildlife parks are resentful because their animals have nowhere to graze. Wasteland development schemes are opposed by nomadic cattlemen and goatherds who claim that the land is their grazing land. With increasing frequency activists are finding themselves in opposite camps.

An interesting example of a clash between two interests occurred in 1989, when environmentalists and bonded labour activists sparred with each other. It may be noted that in the later stages, the government barely featured in the controversy. The protagonists were two groups of activists. In June 1989, the *Indian Express* carried a story by Anil Agarwal of the Centre for Science and Environment (CSE) in which he took the district authorities to task for felling thousands of trees planted by a local organisation in Gopalpur *tehsil* of Alwar district in Rajasthan. The district authorities indignantly replied that the particular plot of land had been earmarked for the rehabilitation of bonded labour. It could not be made over for another purpose under any circumstances. In any case, there were certainly not that many trees, nor of the height mentioned. The Bandhua Mukti Morcha (BMM) then entered the fray in defence of the bonded labour resettled there. The environmentalists argued that the bonded labourers should have been given some other land. The BMM replied that no other land was suitable for cultivation while trees could be planted elsewhere.

As activists slowly came to realise that they were being pitted against each other instead of coming together for a common cause against the big, bad government, they both withdrew, and lowered the heat. But the first stroke of the bell had been tolled. What that incident exposed was the fact that there are very many competing claims for a limited, non-expanding resource, namely land.

Not only are there claims for the diversion of land to *new* uses; without giving in to a single one of these demands we are still faced with the growing pressure of population. In 1901, undivided India (including princely states) was populated by only 28.5 crores or 285 million people. Never in the history of India had this subcontinent crossed the 200 million mark until the onset of British rule. Today, divided India, which is about two-thirds the huge land mass of British India of 1901, holds a teeming population of over 863 million. By the year 2000, we are expected to approach the one billion mark.

The machine as a symbol of scientific and technological advance is certainly not an undiluted blessing but it is not an unmitigated evil either. It has brought us freedom from want, from untimely death, from ignorance and fear of the unknown as embodied in superstitions. It is the progress in medical knowledge that is responsible for increased life expectancy, as well as the teeming population of the world. Science has also helped us to understand the world we live in, including phenomena like avalanches, tornadoes and earthquakes. Unfortunately, we have begun to treat nature lightly and the Old Mother is fast putting us in our place. However, just because we must learn to have a healthy respect for nature's laws, it does not mean that we should opt for the grim, hostile world of our ancestors.

Nor is it a viable alternative. Can we provide the rural life style of the olden days? How good *was* that life style? Can 80 per cent of the people live off the land? Will the holdings be viable? Did all of them own land in the past? Will they not be subjected to the age old social inequities of untouchability, caste, bondage, migration, poverty? Can we clothe or feed this population without using artificial materials, chemical processes and modern techniques? To take but one example, the rural poor cannot afford hand-made cloth. It is the prerogative of the rich and the enlightened activists. Even families with average incomes use mill-made cloth. Can we even give them cooking vessels without exploiting our mineral resources? Can we say 'no' to all change? Or do we expect the majority to agree to do without food, clothing, utensils and even medicines so that we may adhere to the way of life of our ancestors?

Can we provide fuel to our millions from our forests? Will there be any forest left? If we do succeed in abolishing the felling of forests by contractors, who are admittedly an evil, would it save our forests? Do the forest contractors themselves fell the trees or do they hire labourers who badly need the daily wage to feed their families? Many of these men cut trees and take them to the market for sale themselves. Will they be able to stop this activity? An argument against the ban on the export of frog legs has been that the frog catchers will starve. Will the same situation repeat itself if tree cutting is banned?

It is undoubtedly true that government policies are throttling handicrafts and handicraft workers. To the basket weaver, the government sells one bamboo for one rupee. To the paper mill, one ton for 16 rupees. This is true in other areas as well. While the weaver must get cheap bamboo and the paper mills must pay more for the bamboo and we for the paper, it is doubtful whether the closure of paper mills will make the basket weaving industry at once viable and a major supplier of our needs.

If the human population has grown so has the cattle population. Can we afford to graze them in the forests? Rural, as opposed to urban, activists are saying no to many of these questions. Land is brought under grass and then forests by Chipko women and men by preventing the entry of cattle and humans. Annasaheb Hazare of Ralegaon Shindi is staunchly in favour of stall-feeding cattle, for whom grass is grown on allocated land. The villagers in the Shivalik hills were allotted a part of the forest for fodder needs and promptly banned grazing of their cattle in it. They too have opted for stall-feeding and planned fodder-harvesting.

The same is true for fuel as well. Ralegaon Shindi has opted for gobar gas and night soil gas. Chipko women try to procure kerosene and even gas. The Nirdhoom *chulha* which is low on fuel is another alternative that is favoured.

And what of land? In Narmada Valley, the Bhils once complained that it was unfair that only sons who were 18 years of age in the mid-1970s would be entitled to land. What of boys of 11 and 12 who were already ploughing land?

'Let us ask the government to give land to everyone born on the date of displacement,' I said. The men who sat around the fire beamed with delight at the wonderful vision.

'Do you guarantee that no children will be born after that?'

Shouts of laughter greeted my question.'How could that be?'

'Well then, what will you do when you or your sons have children? Will you be able to get more land?'

No, that would not be possible. Here in the forest, they could always encroach a little, pay bribes and endure humiliation at the hands of forest guards. Once they were given revenue land, they would be free of the forest guards but they would not be able to encroach.

'What will you do then?' I said.

'We would have to sub-divide the land'.

'If you divide your five acres between the sons born after displacement, how much will they get?'

'Very little'.

'How much will *their* sons get?'

'Even less'.

'Will they be able to live off the land?'

'Well, not really.'

'What then is the answer?'

Leaning forward, a young teenager interjected, 'hikkan'. i.e., *shikshan* or education.

It is to *this* solution that we, the urban activists, are averse, although ironically we adopted it for ourselves several generations ago. Not one of us follows our caste occupations and the women amongst us have come to occupy the positions that they hold precisely because we abandoned the traditions of our ancestors and took to education, to a way of life that opened up our minds and gave us identities of our own.

As Professor Amartya Sen (1990) has recently pointed out, only 36 per cent of our population is literate. At the same time, as much as 8 per cent of the population in the age group 20 to 24 years takes advantage of higher education, a proportion countries with *twice* our per capita income cannot aspire to emulate. Yet, when it comes to educating the rural poor, we are overcome by doubts. We ask: Can we make education compulsory without punishing default- ing parents? What good will education do? Where are the jobs for them? Will they not be tempted by the modern life style in the cities? Tribals threatened with displacement are clearly being dis- couraged about the utility of education.

Having opted for modernity for ourselves, we are imposing tradition on others. We do so not only without asking them their preference, but also without considering whether the Earth can provide it.

While debating the same point about the need to provide for future generations of oustees, some activists came up with the interesting notion that they should be given land which would enable them to produce a surplus which would sustain *one* more generation. 'What about the second generation?' I asked. Hesitantly, they answered, 'Well, it will have to be education and jobs'. Such thinking betrays an appalling bankruptcy of intellect at the cost of others. We ourselves would spend all our surplus on better living and consider ourselves made poorer in the next generation. Even if it worked, this suggestion would only postpone the evil moment by a few years.

Not only do we expect the rural poor to compete for decreasing land resources by withholding other skills from them, we further deplete those resources by wanting a share larger than our due. Our major and reduceable claim on land and land-based natural resources comes from our increasing consumerism. We behave as though each day was the last for this earth and there was no need to save for tomorrow.

We are claiming resources never claimed by our ancestors in order to achieve a more epicurean life style. Even the average middle income person today lives far better than the very rich of not so long ago. In terms of variety of goods, creature comforts and entertainment, we have far outstripped the most luxurious life styles of the past. Cleopatra might have bathed in asses' milk, drunk pearls dissolved in wine, and sailed the Nile on a barge with silken sails. But the barge was not airconditioned. Her table was not supplied with Indian frogs' legs and she could not take the Concorde to New York for a weekend. Nor could she deplete the ozone layer.

Even here, our campaigns are directed against governments, and not at the consumers who are as responsible for this Earth as anyone else, government or non-government.

There is no doubt that the untramelled consumerism of today *has* to give way. There is also no room for doubt that the need for conservation has to be looked at more seriously and with the utmost urgency. Rather than recklessly exploit the Earth, we must use its resources more economically and frugally. Thus, instead of building more dams, we must learn techniques of water harvesting and stop wasting energy, be it oil, gas, electricity or coal. This is true in all areas. Yet, it will not solve our problem, which arises out of the growing demands of an exploding population. The heartless and massive displacement of our people threatened by development has certainly given a poignant immediacy to a problem that lurks around the corner. But it has not created it. In any event we must tackle the problem of rapidly increasing and competing claims on the Earth and its resources.

Equally, there is no room for doubt that we have to move towards non-land-based occupations. This does not necessarily and only mean more industry. It does mean increased emphasis on labour-intensive modes of production, but also greater diversification of our economy. Even more significant, it means opening up new occupations of knowledge and information gathering, of research as well as welfare services. The middle class has neither the ability nor the time for it. The rural poor do not have the tools. Consequently, to take one example, we have hardly any data on the riverine and forest biology of rivers to be dammed, or on the cultural patterns of people to be displaced. We are left with only vague, romanticised tales.

There is no doubt that given the total lack of advance planning for the displaced populations, land for land is the only viable and just rehabilitation policy for the current generation. But let us not confine future generations to it with no other alternatives.

Not so long ago, some of us were in the Satpuda mountains, in the villages that were to come under submergence by Narmada dams. We were two middle class women, Ujjwala and I. And we spoke Marathi, Hindi and English. Our translator was a Bhil school teacher. Our guides on one lap of the journey were two bright-eyed boys, not yet in their teens. But they ploughed their own fields and were far more capable, confident and fearless than their urban, schoolgoing contemporaries. They spoke only Bhilori, the teacher spoke Bhilori and Marathi. We spoke to him in Marathi and when we desired privacy, resorted to English. To the occasional pilgrim we spoke in Hindi. Young Ujjwala was quick to pick up Bhilori, though she naturally could not speak it. After a few hours of our trek one of the boys remarked to the other, 'These ladies know so many languages. They travel such long distances. If we had been educated, we would have done the same'.

The same and more. Much more. Because we have a need to preserve old cultures, let us not imprison others in them. As it is they will be displaced and the jungle that we call our civilisation will destroy them because they have not the mental equipment to deal with it.

While we try to preserve the culture of the rural populations, we have forgotten our untouchables or scheduled castes. To which culture, to which glorious past do we return them? Is it possible to eradicate prejudices if we continue caste-based occupational patterns in the name of preserving old cultures? This is not a question we can answer with facile ease.

The trees and the wild creatures of land and water cannot migrate or learn new skills. Man is adaptable. If we, the *homo sapiens*, have benefitted through our adaptability and far outstripped our ancestors in knowledge and power, we also have a solemn responsibility to use this talent to save nature, to save the Earth. Of all calls on the use of land, our call *must* come last. Then alone will we save this planet for future generations, for humankind, and indeed, for all that inhabit it.

While this certainly means a drastic reduction in the wasteful consumption of energy and resources by the elite and the privileged, it also means a basic change in the land-use patterns that are no longer suitable in the face of a growing population.

References

Sen, Amartya. 1990. How is India doing? *Indian Express*, 17 June.

Contributors

Kulan Amin: Is a member of 'Kalpvriksh', an environmental group and is currently engaged in a project on organic farming.

Renu Bhanot: Had been working with MARG since 1986. From 1987 onwards, she has been involved with the issues of displacement and rehabilitation.

Vasudha Dhagamwar: Is a law teacher turned legal activist. She has done participatory research on land laws and criminal justice in tribal areas culminating in Supreme Court cases. She has been interested in issues concerning unorganised labour, displacement and rehabilitation of project displaced persons and womens rights. She is the Executive Director of MARG.

Ashish Kothari: Is one of the founding members of 'Kalpvriksh' and is on the faculty of the Indian Institute of Public Administration, New Delhi.

Kashyap Mankodi: Is a Freelance Research Scholar and a part-time World Bank Consultant. Prior to this he has worked in the Centre for Social Studies, Surat and the Centre for Science and Environment, New Delhi.

Machhindra D. Sakate: Is currently a lecturer in sociology at the Rajshri Shahu College, Kolhapur. He takes keen interest in the problems of the Dalits and is actively involved in the Dalit movement.

Ranjan Kumar Samantray: Has been working with MARG since 1988. He has been working on various issues like displacement, rehabilitation, energy and forests. Prior to joining MARG he was working with UNHCR on the rehabilitation of Iranian and Afghan refugees.

Mridula Singh: Has been working with MARG since 1988 and has been involved in research on displacement and rehabilitation. She is currently working on a study on the resettlement of persons displaced by Tehri and Sardar Sarovar Projects.

Shekhar Singh: Is on the faculty of the Indian Institute of Public Administration, New Delhi. He was earlier Honorary Advisor on Environment & Forests to the Planning Commission.

Enakshi Ganguly Thukral: Has been working with MARG since 1986 and has been involved in studies on labour in the unorganised sector, displacement and rehabilitation of project displaced persons. Prior to joining MARG, she was working with the Indian Social Institute.

Kalpana Vaswani: Is an advocate and solicitor who has been doing consultancy work for MARG since 1986. She is currently working on a socio-legal manual for MARG.

Philip Viegas: Is a social psychologist engaged in research on tribals and forests. He is also currently working on his doctoral thesis. Till 1990 he used to be Director, Research, Indian Social Institute, New Delhi.